TEACHER'S PET PUBLICATIONS

LITPLAN TEACHER PACK
for
The Glass Menagerie
based on the play by
Tennessee Williams

Written by
Mary B. Collins

© 1996 Teacher's Pet Publications
All Rights Reserved

This **LitPlan** for Tennessee Williams'
The Glass Menagerie
has been brought to you by Teacher's Pet Publications, Inc.

Copyright Teacher's Pet Publications 1996
11504 Hammock Point
Berlin MD 21811

Only the student materials in this unit plan (such as worksheets,
study questions, and tests) may be reproduced multiple times
for use in the purchaser's classroom.

For any additional copyright questions,
contact Teacher's Pet Publications.

www.tpet.com

TABLE OF CONTENTS - *The Glass Menagerie*

Introduction	5
Unit Objectives	8
Reading Assignment Sheet	9
Unit Outline	10
Study Questions (Short Answer)	13
Quiz/Study Questions (Multiple Choice)	20
Pre-reading Vocabulary Worksheets	33
Lesson One (Introductory Lesson)	43
Nonfiction Assignment Sheet	47
Oral Reading Evaluation Form	50
Writing Assignment 1	52
Writing Assignment 2	59
Writing Assignment 3	63
Writing Evaluation Form	64
Vocabulary Review Activities	56
Extra Writing Assignments/Discussion ?s	54
Unit Review Activities	66
Unit Tests	69
Unit Resource Materials	103
Vocabulary Resource Materials	117

A FEW NOTES ABOUT THE AUTHOR
Tennessee Williams

WILLIAMS, Tennessee (1911-83). The dramas of Tennessee Williams are some of the most moving and powerful ever written for the American stage. His Southern settings and Characters depict a world of human frustration in which sex and violence underlie an atmosphere of superficial, faded gentility. He was born Thomas Lanier Williams on March 26, 1911, in Columbus, Miss. He attended the University of Missouri from 1931 to 1933 and Washington University in Saint Louis (1936-37), where he became interested in writing. Williams worked at it during the Great Depression while employed in a shoe factory. He studied dramatic writing at the University of Iowa, from which he graduated in 1938. Afterward he traveled around the country, working at insignificant jobs and writing short plays that were often produced at community theaters. He won some recognition for 'American Blues' (1939), a group of one-act plays.

Williams continued doing odd jobs, however, until his first real success in 1944: 'The Glass Menagerie', a play about a decadent Southern family living under great emotional tension in a city tenement. The play won the New York Drama Critic's Circle award, as did three more of his plays. His next major play was 'A Streetcar Named Desire' (1947), a study of the mental and moral ruin of a former Southern belle, Blanche Du Bois. Her genteel pretensions are no match for her brutish brother-in-law, Stanley Kowalski. This success was followed by 'Camino Real' (1953), 'Cat on a Hot Tin Roof' (1955), 'Suddenly Last Summer' (l958), 'Sweet Bird of Youth' (1959), and 'Night of the Iguana' (1961). 'A Streetcar Named Desire' and 'Cat on a Hot Tin Roof' were both awarded Pulitzer prizes. In addition to long theater runs, all of these plays were filmed. His novel 'The Roman Spring of Mrs. Stone' (1950) also became a motion picture.

Williams's later writing was compromised by health problems, addiction to alcohol and sleeping pills, and a nervous breakdown. His last plays were not well received. He died in New York City on Feb. 25, 1983.

–Courtesy of Compton's Learning Company

INTRODUCTION

This unit has been designed to develop students' reading, writing, thinking, and language skills through exercises and activities related to *The Glass Menagerie* by Tennessee Williams. It includes twenty lessons, supported by extra resource materials.

The **introductory lesson** introduces students to the idea of hobbies and things to do in one's spare time through a bulletin board activity. Following the introductory activity, students are given a transition to explain how the activity relates to the book they are about to read. Following the transition, students are given the materials they will be using during the unit. They are also given the **unit project assignment** in which they will prepare a presentation about their own hobbies/spare time activities.

The **reading assignments** are divided into segments that could be read orally in one class period, depending on the reading abilities of your students. Students have approximately 15 minutes of pre-reading work to do prior to each reading assignment. This pre-reading work involves reviewing the study questions for the assignment and doing some vocabulary work for 8 to 10 vocabulary words they will encounter in their reading.

The **study guide questions** are fact-based questions; students can find the answers to these questions right in the text. These questions come in two formats: short answer or multiple choice. The best use of these materials is probably to use the short answer version of the questions as study guides for students (since answers will be more complete), and to use the multiple choice version for occasional quizzes. It might be a good idea to make transparencies of your answer keys for the overhead projector.

The **vocabulary work** is intended to enrich students' vocabularies as well as to aid in the students' understanding of the book. Prior to each reading assignment, students will complete a two-part worksheet for approximately 8 to 10 vocabulary words in the upcoming reading assignment. Part I focuses on students' use of general knowledge and contextual clues by giving the sentence in which the word appears in the text. Students are then to write down what they think the words mean based on the words' usage. Part II nails down the definitions of the words by giving students dictionary definitions of the words and having students match the words to the correct definitions based on the words' contextual usage. Students should then have an understanding of the words when they meet them in the text.

After each reading assignment, students will go back and formulate answers for the study guide questions. Discussion of these questions serves as a **review** of the most important events and ideas presented in the reading assignments.

After students complete reading the work, there is a **vocabulary review** lesson which pulls together all of the fragmented vocabulary lists for the reading assignments and gives students a review of all of the words they have studied.

A lesson is devoted to the **extra discussion questions/writing assignments**. These questions focus on interpretation, critical analysis and personal response, employing a variety of thinking skills and adding to the students' understanding of the novel.

There is a **group activity** in which students work in small groups to discuss symbolism and characterization in the novel.

The group activity is followed by a **reports and discussion** session in which the groups share their ideas about the themes with the entire class; thus, the entire class is exposed to information about all of the themes and the entire class can discuss each theme based on the nucleus of information brought forth by each of the groups.

There are three **writing assignments** in this unit, each with the purpose of informing, persuading, or having students express personal opinions. The first assignment is to express personal opinions: students tell about a relationship they have with someone in their families. The second assignment is to persuade: students write a letter to Laura convincing her that she can and should think better of herself and work towards becoming self-sufficient, a letter to Amanda convincing her that Tom needs to go out on his own, or a letter to Jim convincing him to break his engagement with Betty to pursue his attraction to Laura. The third assignment is to inform: students inform you what their project will be about and how they are going to do it.

In addition, there is a **nonfiction reading assignment**. Students are required to read a piece of nonfiction related in some way to *The Glass Menagerie*. After reading their nonfiction pieces, students will fill out a worksheet on which they answer questions regarding facts, interpretation, criticism, and personal opinions. During one class period, students make **oral presentations** about the nonfiction pieces they have read. This not only exposes all students to a wealth of information, it also gives students the opportunity to practice **public speaking**.

The **review lesson** pulls together all of the aspects of the unit. The teacher is given four or five choices of activities or games to use which all serve the same basic function of reviewing all of the information presented in the unit.

The **unit test** comes in two formats: multiple choice or short answer. As a convenience, two different tests for each format have been included. There is also an advanced short answer test for students who need more of a challenge.

There are additional **support materials** included with this unit. The **Unit Resources** section includes suggestions for an in-class library, crossword and word search puzzles related to the novel, and extra vocabulary worksheets. There is a list of **bulletin board ideas** which gives the teacher suggestions for bulletin boards to go along with this unit. In addition, there is a list of **extra class activities** the teacher could choose from to enhance the unit or as a substitution for an exercise the teacher might feel is inappropriate for his/her class. **Answer keys** are located directly after the **reproducible student materials** throughout the unit. The student materials may be reproduced for use in the teacher's classroom without infringement of copyrights. No other portion of this unit may be reproduced without the written consent of Teacher's Pet Publications, Inc.

UNIT OBJECTIVES - *The Glass Menagerie*

1. Through reading *The Glass Menagerie* students will gain a better understanding of family relationships.

2. Students will demonstrate their understanding of the text on four levels: factual, interpretive, critical and personal.

3. Students will consider the importance of having self-confidence and taking the responsibility for one's own success or failure in life.

4. Students will be given the opportunity to practice reading aloud and silently to improve their skills in each area.

5. Students will answer questions to demonstrate their knowledge and understanding of the main events and characters in *The Glass Menagerie* as they relate to the author's theme development.

6. Students will enrich their vocabularies and improve their understanding of the novel through the vocabulary lessons prepared for use in conjunction with the novel.

7. The writing assignments in this unit are geared to several purposes:
    a. To have students demonstrate their abilities to inform, to persuade, or to express their own personal ideas
        Note: Students will demonstrate ability to write effectively to <u>inform</u> by developing and organizing facts to convey information. Students will demonstrate the ability to write effectively to <u>persuade</u> by selecting and organizing relevant information, establishing an argumentative purpose, and by designing an appropriate strategy for an identified audience. Students will demonstrate the ability to write effectively to <u>express personal ideas</u> by selecting a form and its appropriate elements.
    b. To check the students' reading comprehension
    c. To make students think about the ideas presented by the novel
    d. To encourage logical thinking
    e. To provide an opportunity to practice good grammar and improve students' use of the English language.

8. Students will read aloud, report, and participate in large and small group discussions to improve their public speaking and personal interaction skills.

READING ASSIGNMENT SHEET - *The Glass Menagerie*

Date Assigned	Assignment	Completion Date
	Scenes 1-2	
	Scenes 3-6	
	Scene 7	

UNIT OUTLINE - *The Glass Menagerie*

1 Introduction Project Assign. Parts Assign.	2 Practice Parts PV 1-2	3 Read 1-2 PV 3-6	4 Study ?s 1-2 Read 3-6 PV 7	5 Study ?s 3-6 Read 7
6 Study ?s 7 Writing Assignment #1	7 Extra Discussion Questions	8 Vocabulary	9 Group Activity	10 Writing Assignment #2
11 Library	12 Nonfiction Reports	13 Writing Assignment #3	14 Project Presentations	15 Project Presentations
16 Project Presentations	17 Speaker	18 Review	19 Test	

Key: P=Preview Study Questions V=Prereading Vocabulary Worksheets

STUDY GUIDE QUESTIONS

SHORT ANSWER STUDY GUIDE QUESTIONS - *The Glass Menagerie*

Scene 1
1. Identify Amanda Wingfield, Laura Wingfield and Tom Wingfield.
2. Where does the play take place?
3. How does Scene One indicate that Amanda is overbearing and sometimes cruel yet clearly loves her children?

Scene Two
1. Why did Laura quit business college?
2. What was Laura actually doing during the hours she was supposed to be in school?
3. How do you think Amanda knows "... what becomes of unmarried women who aren't prepared to occupy a position"?
4. Why did Jim call Laura "Blue Roses"?
5. Amanda realizes that Laura will not be able to cope with any kind of career. What is her solution for Laura's future?

Scene Three
1. Tom opens the scene as the narrator explaining that there is a specter and a hope hovering over the apartment. What is it?
2. How is Amanda preparing for this gentleman caller?
3. What ignited the argument between Tom and Amanda?
4. Why is Tom mad?
5. Why doesn't Amanda believe Tom goes to the movies?
6. The pieces of the glass menagerie breaking accidentally are symbolic of Laura. Explain how.

Scene Four
1. Who is in a "nailed up coffin" and who found a way out of one?
2. Laura leaves the apartment once and slips on the fire escape. What is Williams symbolically telling us?
3. Tom and Amanda disagree over what the causes of human actions should be. What does Tom think? What does Amanda think?
4. What does Amanda ask of Tom?

Scene Five
1. Amanda is concerned about what aspects of the gentleman caller's character?
2. Why does Tom try to warn Amanda that Laura is not like other girls and not to count on too much from her when Jim calls?
3. What can we gather about Amanda's husband's character? Even though we do not see him in the play, we learn some things about him, things which reflect particularly in Tom and Amanda.

The Glass Menagerie Short Answer Study Guide Page 2

Scene Six
1. Amanda makes both of these statements: "All pretty girls are a trap, a pretty trap, and men expect them to be." "No girl can do worse than put herself at the mercy of a handsome appearance." Explain Amanda's double standard.
2. Give examples showing that Amanda does not understand Laura's feelings of fear.
3. What does Laura do after she opens the door for Tom and Jim?
4. What are Tom's plans for the future?
5. How does Amanda act towards Jim?

Scene Seven
1. Where is Laura?
2. Jim sits on the floor by Laura and talks to her. How does she react?
3. What is the significance of Laura's unicorn?
4. Why does Jim ask Laura to dance?
5. Jim has made Laura feel more normal than she has ever felt. Explain the significance of the unicorn's being broken.
6. Why does Jim kiss Laura?
7. How does Laura react to the kiss?
8. What causes Laura to retreat back into her solitary world?
9. Laura sees Jim as a hero with exceptional capabilities. What is Jim actually?
10. Why does Amanda blame Tom for the evening's failure?

ANSWER KEY: SHORT ANSWER STUDY GUIDE QUESTIONS - *The Glass Menagerie*

Scene 1

1. Identify Amanda Wingfield, Laura Wingfield and Tom Wingfield.
    Amanda is the mother of Tom and Laura. She is worried about her children's future and nags them in an effort to improve their chances for a good position.
    Laura is Amanda's daughter. She is slightly crippled. Her real handicap is her inability to cope with the outside world.
    Tom is Amanda's son who narrates the play. He hates his job and wants adventure.

2. Where does the play take place?
    The play takes place in the Wingfield apartment.

3. How does Scene One indicate that Amanda is overbearing and sometimes cruel yet clearly loves her children?
    Amanda ruins dinner by giving constant directions on how to eat, and she admonishes Tom for smoking too much. She looks forward to gentleman callers for Laura, who has never had any. Amanda shows concern for her children yet doesn't appear to realize that her incessant talk of young prominent men who called on her in her youth is of no benefit to Tom who appears to be not at all like her gentleman callers or to Laura who has never had a gentleman caller.

Scene Two

1. Why did Laura quit business college?
    She was very nervous in class and became physically ill during her first speed test.

2. What was Laura actually doing during the hours she was supposed to be in school?
    She was walking in the park, going to museums, and going to the zoo.

3. How do you think Amanda knows ". . . what becomes of unmarried women who aren't prepared to occupy a position"?
    That was probably her exact position when her husband left her.

4. Why did Jim call Laura "Blue Roses"?
    He misunderstood her when she said she had pleurosis.

5. Amanda realizes that Laura will not be able to cope with any kind of career. What is her solution for Laura's future?
    Laura will marry some nice man.

Scene Three

1. Tom opens the scene as the narrator explaining that there is a specter and a hope hovering over the apartment. What is it?

    There are prospects for a gentleman caller for Laura.

2. How is Amanda preparing for this gentleman caller?

    She is selling magazine subscriptions over the telephone to make extra money to fix up the house.

3. What ignited the argument between Tom and Amanda?

    Amanda returned his novel by D. H. Lawrence to the library because she considered it to be obscene.

4. Why is Tom mad?

    Amanda has taken away from Tom any small privacy he had. He is especially disturbed because he pays all the household bills while she attempts to control every aspect of his life. He is working a job he hates to support his mother and sister, and yet his mother still attempts to control him.

5. Why doesn't Amanda believe Tom goes to the movies?

    She cannot distinguish between the two avenues of escape. For Amanda, there are only two choices for Tom: he can work hard and be respectable or he can sink in vice and immorality. She cannot see that it is possible to escape and not come to a bad end. She wants to control him because she knows what will happen if he does escape as his father did.

6. The pieces of the glass menagerie breaking accidentally are symbolic of Laura. Explain how.

    Laura is always quietly there but never directly involved in the skirmishes between Tom and Amanda. She is the one with the most to lose; her life is the fragile one because she is incapable of fending for herself.

Scene Four

1. Who is in a "nailed up coffin" and who found a way out of one?

    Tom feels as if he is. Tom's father did.

2. Laura leaves the apartment once and slips on the fire escape. What is Williams symbolically telling us?

    She cannot deal in any way with the world outside of her apartment. The thought causes her so much anxiety that she becomes physically sick and weak.

3. Tom and Amanda disagree over what the causes of human actions should be. What does Tom think? What does Amanda think?

   Tom believes man's instinct is that of a hunter, lover and fighter; that these are somehow more purely human drives. Amanda believes that people should govern themselves according to principles of the mind and the spirit. She thinks these ideas are superior to the baser human motives. She equates passionate feelings with animal filth.

4. What does Amanda ask of Tom?

   She wants him to bring a gentleman caller for Laura home from work.

Scene Five

1. Amanda is concerned about what aspects of the gentleman caller's character?

   She wants to know if he drinks and what his position is at work.

2. Why does Tom try to warn Amanda that Laura is not like other girls and not to count on too much from her when Jim calls?

   He knows Amanda expects too much of both Laura and Jim; he is much more realistic and doesn't want his mother to experience too much of a disappointment.

3. What can we gather about Amanda's husband's character? Even though we do not see him in the play, we learn some things about him, things which reflect particularly in Tom and Amanda.

   He was a good looking charmer who drank a bit too much and followed where his instincts led him.

Scene Six

1. Amanda makes both of these statements: "All pretty girls are a trap, a pretty trap, and men expect them to be." "No girl can do worse than put herself at the mercy of a handsome appearance." Explain Amanda's double standard.

   Amanda warns that a girl should not be charmed by a man's appearance but should consider his moral character and especially his ability and steadfastness in being able to provide for a family. On the other hand, she apparently doesn't acknowledge that the deception is just as cruel and deceiving when practiced by a female. Perhaps both she and Mr. Wingfield were both deceived and thus both disappointed.

2. Give examples showing that Amanda does not understand Laura's feelings of fear.

   Amanda fusses over Laura so much that the poor girl becomes even more nervous.
   Amanda says, "You couldn't be satisfied with just sitting home . . ." which is exactly what Laura wants.
   Amanda always brags about her seventeen gentleman callers in one day -- to a daughter who has not had any, thereby making Laura feel more insecure.
   Amanda doesn't give Laura any advice or try to calm her fears; she is too busy preparing for

     Jim as if he were coming to call on her.

3. What does Laura do after she opens the door for Tom and Jim?
     She runs away to another room.

4. What are Tom's plans for the future?
     He has paid his dues to the Merchant Seaman's Union and plans to leave soon.

5. How does Amanda act towards Jim?
     She reverts to her girlish charms and talks incessantly at him.

Scene Seven

1. Where is Laura?
     She is huddled on the sofa, too nervous and sick to join the others for dinner.

2. Jim sits on the floor by Laura and talks to her. How does she react?
     She is nervous at first, but she quickly calms down and begins to enjoy talking with him.

3. What is the significance of Laura's unicorn?
     It is different from all the other animals in the menagerie; likewise, she is different from other girls. It is also the most delicate animal in the collection, as she has the most delicate character in the family.

4. Why does Jim ask Laura to dance?
     He knows she is very shy and insecure. He is trying to make her realize that she is not so different from anyone else.

5. Jim has made Laura feel more normal than she has ever felt. Explain the significance of the unicorn's being broken.
     The unicorn is also now a normal horse and symbolizes that Laura has also become more "normal" during her time with Jim.

6. Why does Jim kiss Laura?
     He is trying hard to make her realize that she is pretty and appealing to men. He is also a bit charmed by her.

7. How does Laura react to the kiss?
     She is dazed and bright-eyed.

8. What causes Laura to retreat back into her solitary world?
     Jim confesses that he is to be married to a girl named Betty.

9. Laura sees Jim as a hero with exceptional capabilities. What is Jim actually?

    He is just a regular man who is kind, a little clumsy, and holds an ordinary job.

10. Why does Amanda blame Tom for the evening's failure?

    She knows she has only herself to blame, but she cannot accept her own failure. She would have to accept some responsibility for both Tom's and Laura's unhappiness.

MULTIPLE CHOICE STUDY GUIDE/QUIZ QUESTIONS - *The Glass Menagerie*

<u>Scene One</u>

1. Amanda is the mother of Tom and Laura. She is worried about her children's future and nags them in an effort to improve their changes for a good position.
    a. True
    b. False

2. Laura wants adventure. She is slightly crippled. Her mother refuses to let her go out, and keeps her a virtual prisoner in the apartment.
    a. True
    b. False

3. Tom is shy and frail. Although he is afraid of coping with the outside world, his mother is forcing him to "be a man" and get a job.
    a. True
    b. False

4. Where does the play take place?
    a. It takes place in Laura's hospital room.
    b. It takes place in Tom's office.
    c. It takes place in the Wingfield apartment.
    d. It takes place in the funeral parlor during Amanda's funeral.

5. In Scene One, Amanda gives constant directions on how to eat dinner, admonishes Tom for smoking too much, and looks forward to gentleman callers for Laura, who has never had any. What do these actions indicate?
    a. Amanda is on the verge of mental collapse.
    b. Amanda is sadistic and cruel to those around her.
    c. Amanda is acting out the treatment she received as a child.
    d. Amanda is overbearing yet clearly loves her children.

The Glass Menagerie Multiple Choice Study Questions Page 2

Scene Two

6. Why did Laura quit business college?
    a. A boy in the class was making passes at her and she got scared.
    b. She was nervous in class and became physically ill during her first speed test.
    c. She was secretly saving the money so she could buy a train ticket to another city.
    d. She did it to defy her mother and show her independence.

7. Laura was actually doing other things during the time she was supposed to be in school. Which of these was she not doing?
    a. She was attending the theater.
    b. She was walking in the park.
    c. She was going to museums.
    d. She was going to the zoo.

8. How do you think Amanda knows,"... what becomes of unmarried women who actually aren't prepared to occupy a position?"
    a. She has been talking to an employment counselor.
    b. She has been reading books about unmarried women and their lives.
    c. That was probably her exact position when her husband left her.
    d. It is the situation that happened to her best friend.

9. Why did Jim call Laura, "Blue Roses"?
    a. He misunderstood her when she said she had pleurosis.
    b. He thought her blue eyes were as pretty as flowers.
    c. It was a thinly-veiled insult. Blue roses are very odd, as he thought she was.
    d. It was the name of her favorite perfume, and she had told him that.

10. Amanda realizes that Laura will not be able to cope with any kind of career. What is her solution for Laura's future?
    a. Amanda files for disability payments for Laura.
    b. Amanda suggests that Laura enter a convent where she will pray all of the time and not have any contact with the outside world.
    c. Amanda encourages Laura to see a therapist and work on the problem.
    d. Amanda thinks Laura should marry a nice man.

The Glass Menagerie Multiple Choice Study Questions Page 3

Scene Three

11. Tom opens the scene as the narrator explaining that there is a specter and a hope hovering over the apartment. What is it?
    a. Laura's father has died and left her a considerable amount of money.
    b. There are prospects for a gentleman caller for Laura.
    c. Tom has been offered a better position in another city. They are all going with him.
    d. Amanda has decided to let Laura live her own life.

12. How is Amanda preparing for this event?
    a. She is studying the stock market.
    b. She is going to Mass twice a day.
    c. She is looking for a job for herself.
    d. She is selling magazine subscriptions to make extra money to fix up the house.

13. What ignited the argument between Tom and Amanda?
    a. Amanda returned his novel by D.H. Lawrence to the library because she considered it to be obscene.
    b. Amanda called Tom's boss and asked him for a raise for Tom.
    c. Amanda is angry because she found out that Tom has a girlfriend. She told him to stop seeing her.
    d. Amanda didn't give him an important letter that he had received from his father.

14. Why is Tom mad?
    a. He is jealous because his mother pays more attention to Laura than to him.
    b. He doesn't want Laura to have any male visitors.
    c. He is working a job he hates to support his mother and sister, and yet his mother still attempts to control him.
    d. He wants Amanda to use the money she is earning to buy him a car, but she won't.

15. Why doesn't Amanda believe Tom goes to the movies?
    a. She is neurotic and afraid that he secretly has a girlfriend.
    b. She has a friend who told her she once saw Tom in a bar when he was supposed to be at the movies.
    c. She cannot see that it is possible to escape and not come to a bad end.
    d. She thinks it is sinful to waste time, and she believes movies are a waste of time.

16. Laura is always quietly there but never directly involved in the skirmishes between Tom and Amanda. She is the one with the most to lose; her life is the fragile one because she is incapable of fending for herself. How is this shown in this act?
    a. She doesn't do much of the talking.
    b. She cries a lot.
    c. The pieces of the glass menagerie break accidentally.
    d. Tom and Amanda are shown as much stronger.

The Glass Menagerie Multiple Choice Study Questions Page 4

Scene Four

17. Who is in the "nailed up coffin" and who found a way out of one?
     a. Laura is in it. Tom got out.
     b. Amanda is in it. Laura got out.
     c. Tom is in it. His father got out.
     d. Laura is in it. Amanda got out.

18. Laura cannot deal in any way with the outside world. The thought causes her so much anxiety that she becomes physically sick and weak. How does Williams symbolically show this?
     a. She keeps her glass collection locked up.
     b. She doesn't own a coat, scarf, or gloves since she never goes out.
     c. She refuses to use the telephone.
     d. She leaves the apartment once and slips on the fire escape.

19. Tom and Amanda disagree over what the causes of human action should be. What does Tom think?
     a. Tom thinks that man is the master of his fate.
     b. Tom thinks that man's course in life is predetermined and cannot be controlled or changed.
     c. Tom thinks man's instinct is that of a hunter, lover and fighter; that these are somehow more purely human drives.
     d. Tom thinks man should be free to do whatever suits him at a given moment.

20. What does Amanda think the causes of human actions should be?
     a. Amanda believes people should govern themselves according to principles of the mind and the spirit. She equates passionate feelings with animal filth.
     b. Amanda believes basically the same things as Tom. He developed his philosophy from her influences.
     c. Amanda believes people should do whatever it takes to survive.
     d. Amanda is very religious. She believes people should follow the Bible's teachings exactly.

21. What does Amanda ask of Tom?
     a. She wants him to either ask for a raise or get another, better paying job. She wants to move to a larger apartment.
     b. She wants him to start taking her and Laura to church every Sunday.
     c. She wants him to bring a gentleman caller for Laura home from work.
     d. She wants him to find a psychiatrist who can help Laura.

The Glass Menagerie Multiple Choice Study Questions Page 5

Scene Five

22. Amanda is concerned about what aspects of the gentleman caller's character?
    a. She wants to know if he drinks and what his position is at work.
    b. She wants to know if he has been married before and if he has any children.
    c. She wants to know if he smokes, if he is religious and to which religion he belongs.
    d. She wants to know if he has a sense of humor and if he is a gambler.

23. Why does Tom try to warn Amanda that Laura is not like the other girls and not to count on too much from her when Jim calls?
    a. He knows that Laura is secretly planning to ruin the evening.
    b. He is really jealous and insecure. He doesn't want anything about their current living arrangement to change.
    c. He is feeling guilty because he knows he deliberately chose a co-worker who would not get along with Laura.
    d. He knows Amanda expects too much of both Laura and Jim; he is much more realistic and doesn't want his mother to experience too much of a disappointment.

24. What can we gather about Amanda's husband's character? Even though we do not see him in the play, we learn some things about him, things which reflect particularly in Tom and Amanda.
    a. He was kind and sweet and unassuming. He was always trying to please others.
    b. He was a good looking charmer who drank a bit too much and followed where his instincts led him.
    c. He was a hard-driving, career-oriented man who cared little for his family.
    d. He was sickly and very much an introvert.

The Glass Menagerie Multiple Choice Study Questions Page 6

Scene Six

25. Amanda makes both of these statement: "All pretty girls are a trap, a pretty trap, and men expect them to be." "No girl can do worse than put herself at the mercy of a handsome appearance." What do these statements show about her?
    a. She is losing her grip on reality.
    b. She is a perfectionist.
    c. She has feelings for her children, even though she doesn't express them clearly.
    d. She has a double standard.

26. Amanda ignores Laura, which hurts her feelings.
    a. This is an example of Amanda's lack of understanding.
    b. This is not an example of Amanda's lack of understanding.

27. "Amanda says, "You couldn't be satisfied with just sitting home..."which is exactly what Laura wants.
    a. This is an example of Amanda's lack of understanding.
    b. This is not an example of Amanda's lack of understanding.

28. Amanda always brags about her seventeen gentleman callers in one day--to a daughter who has not had any, thereby making Laura feel even more insecure.
    a. This is an example of Amanda's lack of understanding.
    b. This is not an example of Amanda's lack of understanding.

29. Amanda gives Laura constant advice and tries to calm her fears.
    a. This is an example of Amanda's lack of understanding.
    b. This is not an example of Amanda's lack of understanding.

30. What does Laura do after she opens the door for Tom and Jim?
    a. She faints.
    b. She starts crying and shaking.
    c. She asks Jim if he would like to play a game.
    d. She runs away to another room.

31. What are Tom's plans for the future?
    a. He is going back to school to work on his doctorate.
    b. He is planning to move to California to break into the movie business.
    c. He has paid his dues to the Merchant Seaman's Union and plans to leave soon.
    d. He wants to become president of the company where he works, so he is working long hours.

The Glass Menagerie Multiple Choice Study Questions Page 7

32. How does Amanda act towards Jim?
    a. She is rude and sarcastic.
    b. She reverts to her girlish charms and talks incessantly at him.
    c. She ignores Jim and talks at him through Laura.
    d. She is very businesslike and aloof.

The Glass Menagerie Multiple Choice Study Questions Page 8

Scene Seven

33. Where is Laura?
    a. She is standing out on the fire escape.
    b. She is huddled on the sofa, too nervous and sick to join the others for dinner.
    c. She is in her bedroom, crying.
    d. She has locked herself in the bathroom.

34. Jim sits on the floor by Laura and talks to her. How does she react?
    a. She is nervous at first, but she quickly calms down and begins to enjoy talking to him.
    b. She smiles but she is so nervous that she picks her nails and doesn't say anything.
    c. She moves to the other side of the room and refuses to look at him.
    d. She cries and shakes, but keeps trying to talk to him.

35. One of Laura's animals is different from all of the others in the menagerie. It symbolizes that she is different from others, and also has the most delicate character in the family. What animal is it?
    a. It is a swan.
    b. It is a fawn.
    c. It is a butterfly.
    d. It is a unicorn.

36. Jim knows that Laura is very shy and insecure. He tries to make her realize that she is not so different from anyone else. What does he do?
    a. He reads poetry to her.
    b. He takes her out to the fire escape to look at the stars.
    c. He asks her to dance.
    d. He tells her about his own troubled childhood.

37. Jim has made Laura feel more normal than she has ever felt. What event in this scene symbolizes this?
    a. They laugh and exchange telephone numbers.
    b. The unicorn's horn breaks off.
    c. Laura shows him her baby pictures.
    d. Jim gets indigestion and needs to lie down.

38. Why does Jim kiss Laura?
    a. He is politely telling her good by.
    b. Tom has paid him to do it.
    c. He is showing his contempt of Amanda and her silly ideas.
    d. He is trying hard to make her realize that she is pretty and appealing to men.

The Glass Menagerie Multiple Choice Study Questions Page 8

39. How does Laura react to the kiss?
    a. She is dazed and bright-eyed.
    b. She is terrified. She slaps him and runs away.
    c. She kisses him back.
    d. She faints in his arms.

40. What causes Laura to retreat back into her solitary world?
    a. He tells her he likes her but can't stand Amanda. He says he won't ask her on a date.
    b. Her mother screams at her for kissing Jim.
    c. Jim makes fun of her collection of animals.
    d. Jim confesses that he is to be married to a girl named Betty.

41. Laura sees Jim as a hero with exceptional capabilities. What is Jim actually?
    a. He is an egotistical playboy.
    b. He is a kind, slightly clumsy man who holds an ordinary job.
    c. He is even more heroic and exceptional than she realizes.
    d. He is an unintelligent, rather slovenly bore.

42. The evening is a failure. What does Amanda do?
    a. She blames Tom.
    b. She screams at Laura for being disabled.
    c. She cries and apologizes to both of them.
    d. She refuses to discuss the matter.

ANSWER KEY - MULTIPLE CHOICE STUDY/QUIZ QUESTIONS
The Glass Menagerie

Scene One	Scene Two	Scene Three
1. A	6. B	11. B
2. B	7. A	12. D
3. B	8. C	13. A
4. C	9. A	14. C
5. D	10. D	15. C
		16. C

Scene Four	Scene Five	Scene Six
17. C	22. A	25. D
18. D	23. D	26. B
19. C	24. B	27. A
20. A		28. A
21. C		29. B
		30. D
		31. C
		32. B

Scene Seven
33. B
34. A
35. D
36. C
37. B
38. D
39. A
40. D
41. B
42. A

PREREADING VOCABULARY WORKSHEETS

Vocabulary - *The Glass Menagerie*

Scenes One and Two Part I: Using Prior Knowledge and Contextual Clues

Below are the sentences in which the vocabulary words appear in the text. Read the sentence. Use any clues you can find in the sentence combined with your prior knowledge, and write what you think the underlined words mean on the lines provided.

1. I reverse it to that quaint period, the thirties, when the huge middle class of America was matriculating in a school for the blind.

   _____

2. He is the most realistic character in the play, being an emissary from a world of reality that we were somehow set apart from.

   _____

3. Animals have secretions in their stomachs which enable them to digest food without mastication, but human beings are supposed to chew their food before they swallow it down.

   _____

4. It wasn't enough for a girl to be possessed of a pretty face and a graceful figure-although I wasn't slighted in either respect.

   _____

5. Amanda leans against the shut door and stares at Laura with a martyred look.

   _____

6. Deliberately courting pneumonia in that light coat?

   _____

7. You did all this to deceive me, just for deception.

   _____

8. I've seen such pitiful cases in the South-barely tolerated spinsters living upon the grudging patronage of sister's husband or brother's wife!-stuck away in some little mousetrap of a room-encouraged by one in-law to visit another-little birdlike women without any nest-eating the crust of humility all their life!

   _____

9. He must have had a jolly disposition.

   _____

33

Glass Menagerie Prereading Vocabulary Worksheet Scenes 1&2 page 2

10. When I had that attack of <u>pleurosis</u>-he asked me what was the matter when I came back.

_____

Part II: Determining the Meaning

You have tried to figure out the meanings of the vocabulary words for Scenes One and Two. Now match the vocabulary words to their dictionary definitions. If there are words for which you cannot figure out the definition by contextual clues and by process of elimination, look them up in a dictionary.

___ 1. matriculating   A. chewing
___ 2. emissary   B. support, encouragement, or championship as of a person, an institution, an event, or a cause from a patron
___ 3. mastication   C. enrolling
___ 4. slighted   D. appeared as one who endures great suffering
___ 5. martyred   E. made small in size, degree, or amount; lacking
___ 6. courting   F. one's usual mood, temperament.
___ 7. deception   G. inflammation of the pleura (lungs), accompanied by fluid in the lungs, chills, fever and painful breathing and coughing
___ 8. patronage   H. an agent sent on a mission to represent or advance the interest of another
___ 9. disposition   I. to behave so as to invite or incur
___10. pleurosis   J. A ruse; a trick

Vocabulary - *The Glass Menagerie* Scene 3 - 6

Part I: Using Prior Knowledge and Contextual Clues

Below are the sentences in which the vocabulary words appear in the text. Read the sentence. Use any clues you can find in the sentence combined with your prior knowledge, and write what you think the underlined words mean on the lines provided.

1. Like some archetype of the universal unconscious, the image of the gentleman caller haunted our small apartment . . . .

_____

2. An evening at home rarely passed without some allusion to this image, this specter, this hope...

_____

3. Yesterday you confiscated my books.

_____

4. Its light on her face with its aged but childish features is cruelly sharp, satirical as a Daumier print.

_____

5. Amanda slips back into her querulous attitude toward him.

_____

6. There is only one respect in which I would like you to emulate your father.

_____

7. Adventure and change were imminent in this year.

_____

8. You're eloquent as an oyster.

_____

9. Preposterous goings on!

_____

10. All vestige of gracious living!

_____

Glass Menagerie Prereading Vocabulary Worksheet Scenes 3-6 page 2

Part II: Determining the Meaning

You have tried to figure out the meanings of the vocabulary words for Scenes 3 - 6. Now match the vocabulary words to their dictionary definitions. If there are words for which you cannot figure out the definition by contextual clues and by process of elimination, look them up in a dictionary.

___ 11. archetype

___ 12. specter

___ 13. confiscated

___ 14. satirical

___ 15. querulous

___ 16. emulate

___ 17. imminent

___ 18. eloquent

___ 19. preposterous

___ 20. vestige

A. Using irony, sarcasm, or caustic wit to attack or expose folly, vice or stupidity

B. given to complaining; peevish

C. about to occur; impending

D. an original model or type after which other similar things are patterned; a prototype

E. a haunting or disturbing image or prospect

F. characterized by persuasive, powerful discourse

G. took

H. contrary to nature, reason or common sense; absurd

I. a visible trace, evidence, or sign of something that once existed but exists or appears no more

J. to strive to equal or excel, especially through imitation

Vocabulary - *The Glass Menagerie* Scene 7

Part I: Using Prior Knowledge and Contextual Clues

Below are the sentences in which the vocabulary words appear in the text. Read the sentence. Use any clues you can find in the sentence combined with your prior knowledge, and write what you think the underlined words mean on the lines provided.

1. There's such a high price for negligence in this world.

   _____

2. I'll give you this lovely old candelabrum that used to be on the altar of the Church of the Heavenly Rest.

   _____

3. Gypsy Jones was holding a revival at the time and he intimated that the church was destroyed because the Episcopalians gave card parties.

   _____

4. I was beleaguered by females in those days.

   _____

5. I know, but I wasn't impressed by that-propaganda!

   _____

6. I had it until I took up public speaking, developed my voice, and learned that I had an aptitude for science.

   _____

7. Mother calls them a glass menagerie!

   _____

8. Tonight I'm rejuvenated!

   _____

9. There is an ominous cracking sound in the sky.

   _____

10. Yes, I know-the tyranny of women!

    _____

Glass Menagerie Prereading Vocabulary Worksheet Scene 7 page 2

Part II: Determining the Meaning

You have tried to figure out the meanings of the vocabulary words for Scene 7. Now match the vocabulary words to their dictionary definitions. If there are words for which you cannot figure out the definition by contextual clues and by process of elimination, look them up in a dictionary.

___ 21. negligence
___ 22. candelabrum
___ 23. intimated
___ 24. beleaguered
___ 25. propaganda
___ 26. aptitude
___ 27. menagerie
___ 28. rejuvenated
___ 29. ominous
___ 30. tyranny

A. menacing; threatening
B. to make known subtly and indirectly; hint
C. a large decorative candlestick having several arms or branches
D. an inherent ability, as for learning, a talent
E. to harass; beset; surrounded by
F. a collection of wild animals on exhibition
G. material disseminated by the advocates of a doctrine or cause
H. to restore to youthful vigor or appearance, make young again
I. extreme harshness or severity; rigor
J. failure to exercise the degree of care considered reasonable under the circumstances

ANSWER KEY - VOCABULARY
The Glass Menagerie

Scenes 1&2	Scenes 3 - 6	Scene 7
1. C	11. D	21. J
2. H	12. E	22. C
3. A	13. G	23. B
4. E	14. A	24. E
5. D	15. B	25. G
6. I	16. J	26. D
7. J	17. C	27. F
8. B	18. F	28. H
9. F	19. H	29. A
10. G	20. I	30. I

DAILY LESSONS

LESSON ONE

Objectives
1. To introduce *The Glass Menagerie* unit.
2. To distribute books and other related materials
3. To make the project assignment for the unit
4. To assign the speaking parts for the unit

NOTE: Prior to this unit you need to have made a bulletin board with background paper and titled: HOBBIES: THINGS WE DO FOR FUN AND RELAXATION. Post colorful pictures on the board of things that represent activities people do for hobbies. Leave ample room for students to do their writing in Activity 1.

Activity #1
Have each student go to the bulletin board and write up one thing he/she does as a hobby. Use different colored markers so the bulletin board will be bright and cheerful.

TRANSITION: "In the play we are going to read, *The Glass Menagerie* by Tennessee Williams, Laura, one of the main characters, has a hobby of collecting glass animals. Thus, the title of the play.

Activity #2
Distribute the materials students will use in this unit. Explain in detail how students are to use these materials.

Study Guides   Students should read the study guide questions for each reading assignment prior to beginning the reading assignment to get a feeling for what events and ideas are important in the section they are about to read. After reading the section, students will (as a class or individually) answer the questions to review the important events and ideas from that section of the book. Students should keep the study guides as study materials for the unit test.

Vocabulary   Prior to reading a reading assignment, students will do vocabulary work related to the section of the book they are about to read. Following the completion of the reading of the book, there will be a vocabulary review of all the words used in the vocabulary assignments. Students should keep their vocabulary work as study materials for the unit test.

Reading Assignment Sheet   You need to fill in the reading assignment sheet to let students know by when their reading has to be completed. You can either write the assignment sheet up on a side blackboard or bulletin board and leave it there for students to see each day, or you can duplicate copies for each student to have. In either case, you should advise students to become very familiar with the reading assignments so they know what is expected of them.

Extra Activities Center   The Unit Resource portion of this unit contains suggestions for an extra library of related books and articles in your classroom as well as crossword and word search puzzles. Make an extra activities center in your room where you will keep these materials for students to use. (Bring the books and articles in from the library and keep several copies of the puzzles on hand.) Explain to students that these materials are available for students to use when they finish reading assignments or other class work early.

Nonfiction Assignment Sheet   Explain to students that they each are to read at least one non-fiction piece from the in-class library at some time during the unit. Students will fill out a nonfiction assignment sheet after completing the reading to help you (the teacher evaluate their reading experiences and to help the students think about and evaluate their own reading experiences.

Books   Each school has its own rules and regulations regarding student use of school books. Advise students of the procedures that are normal for your school.

Activity #3

Distribute the Project Assignment Sheet. Discuss the directions in detail and answer any questions students may have regarding the project. Be sure to tell students when the projects will be due.

Activity #4

On the following page you will find a Reading Parts Assignment Sheet. The sheet has all the names of all the characters needed for speaking parts in each scene of *The Glass Menagerie*. All you need to do is fill in students' names opposite the character names.

Give each student a copy of the Reading Parts Assignment Sheet or just tell each student what his/her assigned part is.

If time remains in this class period, students may begin practicing their parts.

LESSON TWO

Objectives
   1. To give students the opportunity to practice their speaking parts together before they have to do so for the oral reading of the play.
   2. To preview the study questions and vocabulary words for Scenes 1 and 2

Activity #1

Give students about fifteen minutes to preview the study questions and to do the prereading vocabulary worksheet for Scenes 1 and 2.

Activity #2

Students should get together in groups according to the scenes they have been assigned. Together as a group, then, they should practice their speaking parts.

READING PARTS ASSIGNMENT SHEET - *The Glass Menagerie*

SCENE	PART	STUDENT
ONE	NARRATOR	
	TOM	
	AMANDA	
	LAURA	
TWO	NARRATOR	
	LAURA	
	AMANDA	
THREE	NARRATOR	
	TOM	
	AMANDA	
	LAURA	
FOUR	NARRATOR	
	TOM	
	LAURA	
	AMANDA	
FIVE	NARRATOR	
	AMANDA	
	TOM	
SIX	NARRATOR	
	TOM	
	AMANDA	
	LAURA	
	JIM	
SEVEN	NARRATOR	
	JIM	
	AMANDA	
	TOM	
	LAURA	

PROJECT ASSIGNMENT SHEET - *The Glass Menagerie*

PROMPT

Generally speaking, there are certain things people have to do -- sleep, eat, go to work or to school. But that still leaves quite a few hours in the day free. Rather than just sleeping or eating more, people usually find something they like to do -- a hobby. In *The Glass Menagerie*, Laura likes to collect little glass animals. Her brother, Tom, likes to go to the movies. What do you like to do?

ASSIGNMENT

Your assignment is to prepare a five to ten minute presentation about your hobby -- something you like to do in your spare time.

GETTING STARTED

Perhaps you have a collection of some sort: baseball cards, stamps, cans, bottle caps, post cards, etc. Maybe you like to build models, work on cars, listen to music, participate in a sport, or play a musical instrument. Whatever your hobby is or whatever you like to do will be the topic of your presentation. Perhaps there is some hobby you would like to become involved with but have never taken the time to look in to it. Here is your chance. If you want to, you may make your presentation about a hobby you would be interested in acquiring.

SOME SUGGESTIONS

One way to organize your presentation would be to spend a minute or two telling exactly what your hobby is and how one who is interested in it would "get into" that hobby.

Follow that with some examples of your hobby. Show your collection or give a demonstration or give examples of things related to your hobby.

Before you just end your presentation, you should take a few minutes to tell everyone why you like this hobby or activity, what the best points and drawbacks of the hobby/activity are.

REQUIREMENTS

1. Your presentation must last at least five minutes but no longer than ten minutes.

2. You must use some kind of audio or visual aid. For example if you talk about collecting baseball cards, you should have baseball cards to show. If you play a musical instrument, you should be able to show the instrument. If you like music, you should have some examples of the kind of music that interests you. If your hobby is something that cannot be demonstrated or presented in the classroom, you may make a video tape of the appropriate information and present that during your presentation. .

3. You must have completed Writing Assignment 1 prior to making your presentation.

NONFICTION ASSIGNMENT SHEET
(To be completed after reading the required nonfiction article)

Name _____ Date _____

Title of Nonfiction Read _____

Written By _____ Publication Date _____

I. Factual Summary: Write a short summary of the piece you read.

II. Vocabulary
    1. With which vocabulary words in the piece did you encounter some degree of difficulty?

    2. How did you resolve your lack of understanding with these words?

III. Interpretation: What was the main point the author wanted you to get from reading his work?

IV. Criticism
    1. With which points of the piece did you agree or find easy to accept? Why?

    2. With which points of the piece did you disagree or find difficult to believe? Why?

V. Personal Response: What do you think about this piece? <u>OR</u> How does this piece influence your ideas?

LESSON THREE

Objectives
    1. To read scenes 1-2
    2. To give students practice reading orally
    3. To evaluate students' oral reading
    4. To preview the study questions and vocabulary for scenes 3-6

Activity #1

Have students read scenes 1-2 of *The Glass Menagerie* out loud in class by reading the parts they have been assigned. If you have not yet completed an oral reading evaluation for your students this marking period, this would be a good opportunity to do so. A form is included with this unit for your convenience.

Activity #2

Prior to your next class meeting, students should preview the study questions and do the prereading vocabulary worksheet for scenes 3-6. If there is time remaining in this class period after reading scenes 1-2, students may begin this assignment.

LESSON FOUR

Objectives
1. To review the main events and ideas from scenes 1-2
2. To preview the study questions for scene 7
3. To familiarize students with the vocabulary in scene 7
4. To read scenes 3-6

Activity #1
  Give students a few minutes to formulate answers for the study guide questions for scenes 1-2, and then discuss the answers to the questions in detail. Write the answers on the board or overhead transparency so students can have the correct answers for study purposes. Note: It is a good practice in public speaking and leadership skills for individual students to take charge of leading the discussions of the study questions. Perhaps a different student could go to the front of the class and lead the discussion each day that the study questions are discussed during this unit. Of course, the teacher should guide the discussion when appropriate and be sure to fill in any gaps the students leave.

Activity #2
  Have students read scenes 3-6 of *The Glass Menagerie* out loud in class by reading the parts they have been assigned. If you have not yet completed an oral reading evaluation for your students this marking period, this would be a good opportunity to do so. A form is included with this unit for your convenience.

Activity #3
  Prior to your next class meeting, students should preview the study questions and do the prereading vocabulary worksheet for scene 7. If there is time remaining in this class period after reading scenes 3-6, students may begin this assignment.

ORAL READING EVALUATION - *The Glass Menagerie*

Name _____ Class _____ Date _____

SKILL	EXCELLENT	GOOD	AVERAGE	FAIR	POOR
Fluency	5	4	3	2	1
Clarity	5	4	3	2	1
Audibility	5	4	3	2	1
Pronunciation	5	4	3	2	1
_____	5	4	3	2	1
_____	5	4	3	2	1

Total _____   Grade _____

Comments:

LESSON FIVE

Objectives
    1. To review the main events and ideas from scenes 3-6
    2. To read scene 7

Activity #1
    Give students a few minutes to formulate answers for the study guide questions for scenes 3-6, and then discuss the answers to the questions in detail. Write the answers on the board or overhead transparency so students can have the correct answers for study purposes.

Activity #2
    Have students read scene 7 of *The Glass Menagerie* out loud in class by reading the parts they have been assigned. Continue the oral reading evaluations if you are doing that in conjunction with the oral reading.

LESSON SIX

Objectives
    1. To review the main ideas and events from scene 7
    2. To give students the opportunity to practice writing to express personal opinions
    3. To have students look more closely at their own family relationship(s)
    4. To give the teacher the opportunity to evaluate students' writing skills

Activity #1
    Give students a few minutes to formulate answers to the study guide questions for scene 7. Discuss the answers to the questions in detail.

Activity #2
    Distribute Writing Assignment #1 and discuss the directions in detail. Allow the remaining class time for students to complete the assignment. Collect the papers at the end of the class period.

    Follow - Up: After you have graded the assignments, have a writing conference with the students. (This unit schedules one in Lesson Seven.) After the writing conference, allow students to revise their papers using your suggestions and corrections. Give them about three days from the date they receive their papers to complete the revision. I suggest grading the revisions on an A-C-E scale (all revisions well-done, some revisions made, few or no revisions made). This will speed your grading time and still give some credit for the students' efforts.

WRITING ASSIGNMENT #1- *The Glass Menagerie*

PROMPT

The Glass Menagerie is, among other things, a play about family relationships -- a mother who cares about her children's future, a son who feels trapped in his everyday routine, a daughter who cannot cope with the outside world -- and their interactions with each other.

Your assignment is to write a composition about your relationship with one of your family members: your mother or father, a sister or brother, a grandparent, an aunt or uncle, or some friend of the family who is close enough to be considered family.

PREWRITING

One way to begin is to sum up your relationship with that person in one sentence. Then jot down a few reasons why you have chosen to describe your relationship that way. Find a couple of specific examples to show your reasons and jot those down, too. From these notes, you can begin to write your paper.

DRAFTING

Begin with an introductory paragraph in which you introduce your reader to your family member. Lead up to your single sentence which describes your relationship with that person.

The paragraphs in the body of your composition should relate to your reasons why you have chosen to describe your relationship in that way. Write one paragraph for each of your reasons. Use the specific examples you chose to support your reasons.

Your final paragraph will summarize your points and give your final thoughts on the topic.

PROMPT

When you finish the rough draft of your paper, ask a student who sits near you to read it. After reading your rough draft, he/she should tell you what he/she liked best about your work, which parts were difficult to understand, and ways in which your work could be improved. Reread your paper considering your critic's comments, and make the corrections you think are necessary.

PROOFREADING

Do a final proofreading of your paper double-checking your grammar, spelling, organization, and the clarity of your ideas.

LESSON SEVEN

Objective
    To discuss *The Glass Menagerie* on interpretive and critical levels

Activity
    Choose the questions from the Extra Discussion Questions/Writing Assignments which seem most appropriate for your students. A class discussion of these questions is most effective if students have been given the opportunity to formulate answers to the questions prior to the discussion. To this end, you may either have all the students formulate answers to all the questions, divide your class into groups and assign one or more questions to each group, or you could assign one question to each student in your class. The option you choose will make a difference in the amount of class time needed for this activity.

    After students have had ample time to formulate answers to the questions, begin your class discussion of the questions and the ideas presented by the questions. Be sure students take notes during the discussion so they have information to study for the unit test.

LESSON EIGHT

Objectives
To review all of the vocabulary work done in this unit

Activity
    Choose one (or more) of the vocabulary review activities listed after the Extra Discussion Questions and spend your class period as directed in the activity. Some of the materials for these review activities are located in the Vocabulary Resource section in this unit.

EXTRA WRITING ASSIGNMENTS/DISCUSSION QUESTIONS - *The Glass Menagerie*

<u>Interpretation</u>

1. What are the main conflicts in the story? Are they resolved by the end of the play? If so, how? If not, why not?

2. Is the story of *The Glass Menagerie* believable? Explain why or why not.

3. Where is the climax of the story? Explain your choice.

4. Are the characters in *The Glass Menagerie* stereotypes? If so, explain the usefulness of employing stereotypes in the novel. If they are not, explain how they merit individuality.

5. What is the setting of the story? Could this story have been set in a different time and place and still have the same effect?

<u>Critical</u>

6. Explain how Laura and Tom dealt with their mother's nagging. Could they have dealt with it better?

7. Who was responsible for Laura's not having any gentleman callers?

8. Characterize Tennessee Williams's style of writing. How does it contribute to the value of the novel?

9. Was Jim's visit a positive or negative experience for Laura. Would she have been better off in the long run with or without his visit?

10. Explain how the title, *The Glass Menagerie*, is appropriate.

11. Could anything have been gained by adding more scenes to the play? If so, what could have been added and for what purpose.

12. Could *The Glass Menagerie* be considered a tragedy?

13. Explain why Tom left.

14. Does this play have a main character? Justify your answer.

15. What were two main themes in the play?

The Glass Menagerie Extra Discussion Questions page 2

Personal Response

16. Did you enjoy reading *The Glass Menagerie*? Why or why not?

17. Amanda could not understand Laura's fears. Why do you think parents sometimes have a hard time understanding their children? Why do children sometimes have a hard time understanding their parents?

18. Define "handicapped" as it relates to the play.

19. Do you know anyone like any of the characters in the play? If so, who and in what ways are they similar to the character? (Please use a false name for the person so no one will be embarrassed if it is someone others in the class may know.)

20. How is reading a play different from reading a novel? Which do you prefer? Why?

VOCABULARY REVIEW ACTIVITIES

1. Divide your class into two teams and have an old-fashioned spelling or definition bee.

2. Give each of your students (or students in groups of two, three or four) a *Glass Menagerie* Vocabulary Word Search Puzzle. The person (group) to find all of the vocabulary words in the puzzle first wins.

3. Give students a *Glass Menagerie* Vocabulary Word Search Puzzle without the word list. The person or group to find the most vocabulary words in the puzzle wins.

4. Use a *Glass Menagerie* Vocabulary Crossword Puzzle. Put the puzzle onto a transparency on the overhead projector (so everyone can see it), and do the puzzle together as a class.

5. Give students a *Glass Menagerie* Vocabulary Matching Worksheet to do.

6. Divide your class into two teams. Use the *Glass Menagerie* vocabulary words with their letters jumbled as a word list. Student 1 from Team A faces off against Student 1 from Team B. You write the first jumbled word on the board. The first student (1A or 1B) to unscramble the word wins the chance for his/her team to score points. If 1A wins the jumble, go to student 2A and give him/her a definition. He/she must give you the correct spelling of the vocabulary word which fits that definition. If he/she does, Team A scores a point, and you give student 3A a definition for which you expect a correctly spelled matching vocabulary word. Continue giving Team A definitions until some team member makes an incorrect response. An incorrect response sends the game back to the jumbled-word face off, this time with students 2A and 2B. Instead of repeating giving definitions to the first few students of each team, continue with the student after the one who gave the last incorrect response on the team. For example, if Team B wins the jumbled-word face-off, and student 5B gave the last incorrect answer for Team B, you would start this round of definition questions with student 6B, and so on. The team with the most points wins!

7. Have students write a story in which they correctly use as many vocabulary words as possible. Have students read their compositions orally! Post the most original compositions on your bulletin board!

LESSON NINE

<u>Objectives</u>
1. To study the play more closely through all seven scenes
2. To give students the opportunity to practice their personal interaction skills in a small group
3. To give students the opportunity to practice their public speaking skills as they report their small group findings
4. To study the character relationships in *The Glass Menagerie*

<u>Activity</u>
Divide the class into eight groups, one for each of the following topics:

1. The use of Tom as a narrator
2. The relationship between Tom and Amanda
3. The relationship between Tom and Laura
4. The relationship between Laura and Amanda
5. The relationship between Laura and Jim
6. The relationship between Jim and Amanda
7. Reality vs. dreams and/or illusions
8. Symbolism used in the play

Give the group members time to look through the play for specific references to their topics and time to discuss their findings with each other after that. Students should divide the work load up by assigning one or two scenes to each member of the group to find the textual references. One member of the group should be appointed as spokesperson to relate the group's ideas to the class.

After the groups have had ample time to gather their ideas, have each group's spokesperson relate the group's ideas and use that as a springboard for a class discussion of the topics.

LESSON ELEVEN

<u>Objectives</u>
    1. To give students the opportunity to practice writing to persuade
    2. To expand and evaluate students' understanding of the characters in the book
    3. To give the teacher the opportunity to evaluate students' writing skills

<u>Activity</u>
    Distribute Writing Assignment #2. Discuss the directions in detail and give students ample time to complete the assignment.

WRITING ASSIGNMENT #2 - *The Glass Menagerie*

PROMPT

Now that you have completed reading *The Glass Menagerie* and have spent some time talking about the characters, you should pretty well understand the characters, their attitudes, and the things that motivate them.

Your assignment is to write one of the following letters:
1. Convince Laura that she can and should think better of herself and work towards becoming self-sufficient.
2. Convince Amanda that Tom needs to go out on his own.
3. Convince Jim to break his engagement to Betty to pursue his attraction to Laura.

PREWRITING

Choose which of the letters you think you would like to write. Think about the person to whom you are writing. Jot down a list of three or four things that would be most likely to persuade that person to do what you want him/her to do. Which of those things would make your best argument (would be most likely to persuade the person)? Put a star next to that one. Number the remaining items on your list from most persuasive to least persuasive.

DRAFTING

Begin your composition in a letter format. Use the introductory paragraph to introduce the idea you wish to convey in your letter.

In the body of your letter, write one paragraph for each of your persuasive arguments. Some people prefer to write from the least persuasive to the most persuasive arguments. Others prefer to begin with the most persuasive argument and then work from the least persuasive to the second most persuasive arguments. How do you decide which to do? Consider your arguments and your audience. What do you think will work best in your particular situation? After careful consideration, write your paper with the organization you think best suits your situation.

Your closing paragraph could be done in a number of ways. You might give your final thoughts or make a final pitch or plea. You could end either firmly or with a more mellow tone. If your entire letter has been firm, consider whether you should keep that tone or write a few lines in a more mellow tone. The way you will close your letter will depend entirely on you and the impression with which you want to leave your reader.

PROOFREADING

When you finish the rough draft of your paper, ask a student who sits near you to read it. After reading your rough draft, he/she should tell you what he/she liked best about your work, which parts were difficult to understand, and ways in which your work could be improved. Reread your paper considering your critic's comments, and make the corrections you think are necessary. Do a final proofreading of your paper double-checking your grammar, spelling, organization, and the clarity of your ideas.

LESSON ELEVEN

Objective

    To give students the time and opportunity to complete their nonfiction reading assignment

Activity

    Take students to the library so they can find articles or books about nonfiction topics related to *The Glass Menagerie* so they can fulfill their nonfiction reading assignment requirement for the unit.

    Some suggested topics are:
- psychology
- pleurosis and other diseases that cause handicaps
- handicapped people in our society; what we do for them and how they are able to function in society
- employment laws regarding handicapped people
- opportunities for women who choose not to depend on a "gentleman caller"
- secretarial careers or careers in the services -- or other careers
- positive ways to escape the pressures of everyday life
- current plays playing on Broadway (or off-Broadway)
- critical reviews of *The Glass Menagerie*
- movie reviews
- parenting
- ways parents and their kids can bridge the "generation gap"

LESSON TWELVE

Objective
    1. To widen the breadth of students' knowledge about the topics discussed or touched upon in *The Glass Menagerie*
    2. To check students' nonfiction reading assignments

Activity

    Ask each student to give a brief oral report about the nonfiction work he/she read for the nonfiction reading assignment. Your criteria for evaluating this report will vary depending on the level of your students. You may wish for students to give a complete report without using notes of any kind, or you may want students to read directly from a written report, or you may want to do something in between these two extremes. Just make students aware of your criteria in ample time for them to prepare their reports.

    Start with one student's report. After that, ask if anyone else in the class has read on a topic related to the first student's report. If no one has, choose another student at random. After each report, be sure to ask if anyone has a report related to the one just completed. That will help keep a continuity during the discussion of the reports.

LESSON THIRTEEN

Objectives
> 1. To give students the opportunity to practice writing to inform
> 2. To help students prepare for their project presentations
> 3. To give the teacher the opportunity to evaluate students' writing

Activity

Distribute Writing Assignment #3 and discuss the directions in detail. Give students the entire class period to work on this assignment, and then collect the papers for grading.

NOTE:

While students are working on Writing Assignment #3, call individual students to your desk or some other private area for individual writing conferences based on the first two writing assignments in this unit. An evaluation form is included in this unit for your convenience.

LESSONS FOURTEEN - SIXTEEN

Objectives
> 1. To show students that there are many constructive ways to spend their spare time
> 2. To show students how to "get into" a hobby or activity if they find something that interests them
> 3. To give students the opportunity to practice public speaking
> 4. To give students the opportunity to take pride in their spare time activities and to show them off to their classmates
> 5. To help build students' self-confidence

Activity

Have students each make their presentations about their hobbies or spare time activities. The amount of time this takes will depend on the number of students you have and the amount of time each student takes with his/her report. We have allowed three class periods.

WRITING ASSIGNMENT #3 - *The Glass Menagerie*

PROMPT
During the next several class periods you will be giving your presentations about your hobbies. You should already have a pretty good idea what you are going to do and should have all of your materials ready. As a last preparation for the presentation, your assignment is to write a composition in which you give a written form of the information you will give orally in your presentation. This will help you get your information and organization planted in your head before you stand up in front of the class.

PREWRITING
How are you going to start your presentation? Are you going to stand up and give background information about your hobby, follow that with a demonstration and your comments about the pros and cons of your hobby? Perhaps you would rather start with a demonstration and then give the background information followed by the comments about the pros and cons of your hobby. What have you thought about and planned so far?

Make a little outline of what you are going to do for your presentation and the order in which you will do it.

DRAFTING
Working from your outline, write your composition explaining to me what you are going to say and do for your presentation.

In your introductory paragraph introduce the topic about which your presentation will be made.

In the paragraphs in the body of your composition, explain what you are going to say and do in your presentation.

Write a concluding paragraph in which you express any concerns about your presentation.

PROMPT
When you finish the rough draft of your paper, ask a student who sits near you to read it. After reading your rough draft, he/she should tell you what he/she liked best about your work, which parts were difficult to understand, and ways in which your work could be improved. Reread your paper considering your critic's comments, and make the corrections you think are necessary.

PROOFREADING
Do a final proofreading of your paper double-checking your grammar, spelling, organization, and the clarity of your ideas.

WRITING EVALUATION FORM - *The Glass Menagerie*

Name _____ Date _____

    Grade _____

Circle One For Each Item:

Grammar: excellent   good   fair   poor

Spelling: excellent   good   fair   poor

Punctuation: excellent   good   fair   poor

Legibility: excellent   good   fair   poor

Strengths:

Weaknesses:

Comments/Suggestions:

LESSON SEVENTEEN

Objective
1. To help students realize the importance of having confidence in themselves
2. To motivate students to take responsibility for their own lives
3. To show students ways they can help themselves improve their own self-confidence and the self-confidence of others around them

NOTE: Prior to this lesson you need to have invited a guest speaker to discuss the topics mentioned above in the objectives. There are many good, motivational speakers who can address this topic. Check in your local area for a qualified person.

Activity

Introduce the guest speaker and give him/her most of the class period to make a presentation. Try to allow time for a question and answer session between your students and the guest speaker.

LESSON EIGHTEEN

Objective
To review the main ideas presented in *The Glass Menagerie*

Activity #1

Choose one of the review games/activities included in this guide and spend your class period as outlined there. Some materials for these activities are located in the Unit Resource section of this unit.

Activity #2

Remind students that the Unit Test will be in the next class meeting. Stress the review of the Study Guides and their class notes as a last minute, brush-up review for homework.

REVIEW GAMES/ACTIVITIES - *The Glass Menagerie*

1. Ask the class to make up a unit test for *The Glass Menagerie*. The test should have 4 sections: matching, true/false, short answer, and essay. Students may use 1/2 period to make the test and then swap papers and use the other 1/2 class period to take a test a classmate has devised. (open book) You may want to use the unit test included in this guide or take questions from the students' unit tests to formulate your own test.

2. Take 1/2 period for students to make up true and false questions (including the answers). Collect the papers and divide the class into two teams. Draw a big tic-tac-toe board on the chalk board. Make one team X and one team O. Ask questions to each side, giving each student one turn. If the question is answered correctly, that students' team's letter (X or O) is placed in the box. If the answer is incorrect, no mark is placed in the box. The object is to get three marks in a row like tic-tac-toe. You may want to keep track of the number of games won for each team.

3. Take 1/2 period for students to make up questions (true/false and short answer). Collect the questions. Divide the class into two teams. You'll alternate asking questions to individual members of teams A & B (like in a spelling bee). The question keeps going from A to B until it is correctly answered, then a new question is asked. A correct answer does not allow the team to get another question. Correct answers are +2 points; incorrect answers are -1 point.

4. Have students pair up and quiz each other from their study guides and class notes.

5. Give students a *Glass Menagerie* crossword puzzle to complete.

6. Divide your class into two teams. Use the *Glass Menagerie* crossword words with their letters jumbled as a word list. Student 1 from Team A faces off against Student 1 from Team B. You write the first jumbled word on the board. The first student (1A or 1B) to unscramble the word wins the chance for his/her team to score points. If 1A wins the jumble, go to student 2A and give him/her a clue. He/she must give you the correct word which matches that clue. If he/she does, Team A scores a point, and you give student 3A a clue for which you expect another correct response. Continue giving Team A clues until some team member makes an incorrect response. An incorrect response sends the game back to the jumbled-word face off, this time with students 2A and 2B. Instead of repeating giving clues to the first few students of each team, continue with the student after the one who gave the last incorrect response on the team. For example, if Team B wins the jumbled-word face-off, and student 5B gave the last incorrect answer for Team B, you would start this round of clue questions with student 6B, and so on. The team with the most points wins!

UNIT TESTS

SHORT ANSWER UNIT TEST 1 - *The Glass Menagerie*

I. Short Answer

1. Describe the relationship between Amanda and Tom.

2. Describe the relationship between Amanda and Laura.

3. How does Scene One indicate that Amanda is overbearing and sometimes cruel and yet clearly loves her children?

4. How do you think Amanda knows ". . . what becomes of unmarried women who aren't prepared to occupy a position"?

5. Amanda realizes that Laura will not be able to cope with any kind of a career. What is her solution for Laura's future?

6. Of what is the breaking of the unicorn symbolic?

7. Tom and Amanda disagree about what the causes of human action should be. What does Tom think? What does Amanda think?

Glass Menagerie Short Answer Unit Test 1 Page 2

8. How does Laura react to Jim when he arrives and during his visit?

9. Why does Amanda blame Tom for the failure of the evening?

10. Why does Tom leave?

II. Composition

    Tennessee Williams wrote *The Glass Menagerie* about fifty years ago, and yet we are still reading it. What things in or about the play make it a classic?

Glass Menagerie Short Answer Unit Test 1 Page 3

III. Vocabulary

Listen to the vocabulary words and write them down. Go back later and fill in the correct definition for each word.

1.

2.

3.

4.

5.

6.

7.

8.

9.

10.

KEY: SHORT ANSWER UNIT TEST #1 - *The Glass Menagerie*

I. Short Answer

1. Describe the relationship between Amanda and Tom.

    Amanda wants Tom to be a good man, to be able to support a family and to be of good moral character. She is afraid he will turn out like his father. What she doesn't realize is that by nagging and pushing him and being so demanding of him, she forces him to feel the need to escape. She almost pushes him to be the man she doesn't want him to be. Tom wants to be a good man, and he tries very hard to maintain his position, but it finally becomes just too much for him and he has to leave. Tom resents his mother's nagging.

2. Describe the relationship between Amanda and Laura.

    Amanda wants Laura to have a secure future, either by (preferably) having her own career or (when that seems impossible) by having a good man to take care of her. Again, in having such strong desires for her child, Amanda ruins the girl in the process. Instead of being understanding and trying to work with Laura's fears and frustrations, she overlooks them and boldly pushes on toward her final goals. Laura, already insecure, gets totally overwhelmed in the process. Laura is a peacekeeper; she doesn't want to argue with her mother; she just withdraws more into her own world.

3. How does Scene One indicate that Amanda is overbearing and sometimes cruel and yet clearly loves her children?

    Amanda ruins dinner by giving constant directions on how to eat, and she admonishes Tom for smoking too much. She looks forward to a gentleman caller for Laura, who has never had any. Amanda shows concern for her children yet doesn't appear to realize that her incessant talk of young prominent men who called on her in her youth is of no benefit to Tom who appears to be not at all like her gentleman callers or to Laura who has never had a gentleman caller.

4. How do you think Amanda knows ". . . what becomes of unmarried women who aren't prepared to occupy a position"?

    That was probably her exact position when her husband left her.

5. Amanda realizes that Laura will not be able to cope with any kind of a career. What is her solution for Laura's future?

    Laura will marry some nice man who can take care of her.

6. Of what is the breaking of the unicorn symbolic?

    The unicorn's horn makes it different from the other horses in the collection. Likewise, Laura is different from other girls. When the unicorn's horn is broken, it is symbolic of Laura's feeling "normal" in Jim's company.

7. Tom and Amanda disagree about what the causes of human action should be. What does Tom think? What does Amanda think?

   Tom thinks men should live using their instincts and emotions. Amanda thinks men should live by their intellect and reason, "above" their baser instincts.

8. How does Laura react to Jim when he arrives and during his visit?

   Laura is so nervous that she is ill when he first arrives and through dinner. After dinner, he sits down and talks with her and she begins to feel more at ease, almost "normal." After she learns that he is engaged to be married, she reverts back to her own little world, terribly disappointed.

9. Why does Amanda blame Tom for the failure of the evening?

   She blames him so she will not have to be responsible for it. He warned her not to get her hopes up too high, but she ignored him and built up her fantasy of Jim and Laura living happily ever after. When things don't work out, she blames Tom for not knowing Jim was engaged.

10. Why does Tom leave?

    Tom leaves so he can live his own life without his nagging mother.

II. Composition

   Tennessee Williams wrote *The Glass Menagerie* about fifty years ago, and yet we are still reading it. What things in or about the play make it a classic? Answers will vary.

III. Vocabulary

   Choose ten of the vocabulary words. Read them orally to your class so the students can write them down on part IV of their vocabulary tests.

SHORT ANSWER UNIT TEST 2 - *The Glass Menagerie*

I. Short Answer

1. Each of the three main characters has a problem. Identify each of the three main characters and tell what each one's problem is.

2. Why did Laura quit business college?

3. Tom explains that there is a specter and a hope hovering over the apartment. What is it?

4. Why doesn't Amanda believe Tom goes to the movies?

5. The pieces of the glass menagerie breaking accidentally are symbolic of Laura. Explain how.

The Glass Menagerie Short Answer Unit Test 2 Page 2

6. Laura leaves the apartment once and slips on the fire escape. What is Williams symbolically telling us?

7. Tom and Amanda disagree over what the causes of human actions should be. What does Tom think? What does Amanda think?

8. Amanda makes both of these statements: "All pretty girls are a trap, a pretty trap, and men expect them to be." "No girl can do worse than put herself at the mercy of a handsome appearance." Explain Amanda's double standard.

9. Give examples showing that Amanda does not understand Laura's feelings of fear.

10. What is the significance of Laura's unicorn?

11. Laura sees Jim as a hero with exceptional capabilities. What is Jim actually?

The Glass Menagerie Short Answer Unit Test 2 Page 3

II. Composition
    Explain the conflict of illusion vs. reality as it relates to *The Glass Menagerie*.

III. Vocabulary
    Listen to the vocabulary words and write them down. Go back later and fill in the correct definition for each word.

1.

2.

3.

4.

5.

6.

7.

8.

9.

10.

KEY: SHORT ANSWER UNIT TEST 2 *The Glass Menagerie*

I. Short Answer

1. Each of the three main characters has a problem. Identify each of the three main characters and tell what each one's problem is.

    Amanda, mother of Tom and Laura, had devoted her life to her children and in the process has become overbearing and nagging with them. She is overly concerned about Laura's future.
    Laura, Amanda's daughter, is slightly crippled but her real handicap is her lack of self-confidence and her lack of ability to deal with the outside world.
    Tom, Amanda's son, works at a job he doesn't like and considers his life with his nagging mother miserable.

2. Why did Laura quit business college?

    She was very nervous in class and became physically ill during her first speed test.

3. Tom explains that there is a specter and a hope hovering over the apartment. What is it?

    There are prospects for a gentleman caller for Laura.

4. Why doesn't Amanda believe Tom goes to the movies?

    She cannot distinguish between the two avenues of escape. For Amanda, there are only two choices for Tom: he can work hard and be respectable or he can sink in vice and immorality. She cannot see that it is possible to escape and not come to a bad end. She wants to control him because she knows what will happen if he does escape as his father did.

5. The pieces of the glass menagerie breaking accidentally are symbolic of Laura. Explain how.

    Laura is always quietly there but never directly involved in the skirmishes between Tom and Amanda. She is the one with the most to lose; her life is the fragile one because she is incapable of fending for herself.

6. Laura leaves the apartment once and slips on the fire escape. What is Williams symbolically telling us?

    She cannot deal in any way with the world outside of her apartment. The thought causes her so much anxiety that she becomes physically sick and weak.

7. Tom and Amanda disagree over what the causes of human actions should be. What does Tom think? What does Amanda think?

    Tom believes man's instinct is that of a hunter, lover and fighter; that these are somehow more purely human drives. Amanda believes that people should govern themselves according to principles of the mind and the spirit. She thinks these ideas are superior to the baser human motives. She equates passionate feelings with animal filth.

8. Amanda makes both of these statements: "All pretty girls are a trap, a pretty trap, and men expect them to be." "No girl can do worse than put herself at the mercy of a handsome appearance." Explain Amanda's double standard.

> Amanda warns that a girl should not be charmed by a man's appearance but should consider his moral character and especially his ability and steadfastness in being able to provide for a family. On the other hand, she apparently doesn't acknowledge that the deception is just as cruel and deceiving when practiced by a female. Perhaps both she and Mr. Wingfield were both deceived and thus both disappointed.

9. Give examples showing that Amanda does not understand Laura's feelings of fear.

> *Amanda fusses over Laura so much that the poor girl becomes even more nervous.
>
> * Amanda says, "You couldn't be satisfied with just sitting home . . ." which is exactly what Laura wants.
>
> *Amanda always brags about her seventeen gentleman callers in one day -- to a daughter who has not had any, thereby making Laura feel more insecure.
>
> *Amanda doesn't give Laura any advice or try to calm her fears; she is too busy preparing for Jim as if he were coming to call on her.

10. What is the significance of Laura's unicorn?

> It is different from all the other animals in the menagerie; likewise, she is different from other girls. It is also the most delicate animal in the collection, as she has the most delicate character in the family. After breaking, the unicorn is now a normal horse and symbolizes that Laura has also become more "normal" during her time with Jim.

11. Laura sees Jim as a hero with exceptional capabilities. What is Jim actually?

> He is just a regular man who is kind, a little clumsy, and holds an ordinary job.

II. Composition

Explain the conflict of illusion vs. reality as it relates to *The Glass Menagerie*.

III. Vocabulary

Choose ten vocabulary words and read them orally to your class so students can write them down.

ADVANCED SHORT ANSWER UNIT TEST - *The Glass Menagerie*

I. Short Answer

1. Amanda makes both of these statements: "All pretty girls are a trap, a pretty trap, and men expect them to be." "No girl can do worse than put herself at the mercy of a handsome appearance." Explain Amanda's double standard.

2. Each of the three main characters has a problem. Identify each of the three main characters and tell what each one's problem is.

3. Was Jim's visit a positive or negative experience for Laura? Would she have been better off in the long run with or without his visit?

4. Does this play have a main character? Justify your answer.

The Glass Menagerie Advanced Short Answer Unit Test Page 2

5. What were two main themes in the play?

6. Identify two main symbols in the play and explain of what each was symbolic.

7. Explain the significance of the title of the play.

8. Compare Tom to his father.

9. Explain the conflict of illusion vs. reality as it relates to *The Glass Menagerie*.

The Glass Menagerie Advanced Short Answer Unit Test Page 3

III. Composition
    Who felt responsible for Laura? Whose responsibility was Laura's future?

The Glass Menagerie Advanced Short Answer Unit Test Page 4

III. Vocabulary

Write down the vocabulary words you are given. Go back later and use all of those vocabulary words in a composition relating to *The Glass Menagerie*.

MULTIPLE CHOICE UNIT TEST 1 - *The Glass Menagerie*

I. Multiple Choice

1. Amanda is the mother of Tom and Laura. She is worried about her children's future and nags them in an effort to improve their chances for a good position.
    a. True
    b. False

2. Laura wants adventure. She is slightly crippled. Her mother refuses to let her go out, and keeps her a virtual prisoner in the apartment.
    a. True
    b. False

3. Tom is shy and frail. Although he is afraid of coping with the outside world, his mother is forcing him to "be a man" and get a job.
    a. True
    b. False

4. Tom explains that there is a specter and a hope hovering over the apartment. What is it?
    a. Laura's father has died and left her a considerable amount of money.
    b. There are prospects for a gentleman called for Laura.
    c. Tom has been offered a better position in another city. They are all going to move with him.
    d. Amanda has decided to let Laura live her own life.

5. Why doesn't Amanda believe Tom goes to the movies?
    a. She is neurotic and afraid that he secretly has a girlfriend.
    b. She has a friend who told her she once saw Tom in a bar when he was supposed to be at the movies.
    c. She cannot see that it is possible to escape and not come to a bad end.
    d. She thinks it is sinful to waste time, and she doesn't want to believe he is wasting his time and sinning.

6. Who is in the "nailed up coffin" and who found a way out of one?
    a. Laura is in it. Tom got out.
    b. Amanda is in it. Laura got out.
    c. Tom is in it. His father got out.
    d. Laura is in it. Amanda got out.

The Glass Menagerie Multiple Choice Unit Test 1 Page 2

7. Laura cannot deal in any way with the outside world. The thought causes her so much anxiety that she becomes physically sick and weak. How does Williams symbolically show this?
    a. She keeps her glass collection locked up.
    b. She doesn't own a coat, scarf, or gloves since she never goes out.
    c. She refuses to use the telephone.
    d. She leaves the apartment once and slips on the fire escape.

8. Tom and Amanda disagree over what the causes of human action should be. What does Tom think?
    a. Tom thinks that man is the master of his fate.
    b. Tom thinks that man's course in life is predetermined and cannot be controlled or changed.
    c. Tom thinks man's instinct is that of a hunter, lover and fighter; that these are somehow more purely human drives.
    d. Tom thinks man should be free to do whatever suits him at a given moment.

9. What does Amanda think the causes of human actions should be?
    a. Amanda believes people should govern themselves according to principles of the mind and the spirit. She equates passionate feelings with animal filth.
    b. Amanda believes basically the same things as Tom. He developed his philosophy from her influences.
    c. Amanda believes people should do whatever they have to do to survive.
    d. Amanda is very religious. She believes people should follow the Bible's teachings.

10. What does Amanda ask of Tom?
    a. She wants him to either ask for a raise or get another, better paying job. She wants to move to a larger apartment.
    b. She wants him to start taking her and Laura to church every Sunday.
    c. She wants him to bring a gentleman caller for Laura home from work.
    d. She wants him to find a psychiatrist who can help Laura.

11. What can we gather about Amanda's husband's character? Even though we do not see him in the play, we learn some things about him, things which reflect particularly in Tom and Amanda.
    a. He was kind and sweet and unassuming. He was always trying to please others.
    b. He was a good looking charmer who drank a bit too much and followed where his instincts led him.
    c. He was a hard-driving, career-oriented man who cared little for his family.
    d. He was sickly and very much an introvert.

The Glass Menagerie Multiple Choice Unit Test 1 Page 3

12. Amanda makes both of these statement: "All pretty girls are a trap, a pretty trap, and men expect them to be." "No girl can do worse than put herself at the mercy of a handsome appearance." What do these statements show about her?
    a. She is losing her grip on reality.
    b. She is a perfectionist.
    c. She has feelings for her children, even though she doesn't express them clearly.
    d. She has a double standard.

13. What does Laura do after she opens the door for Tom and Jim.
    a. She faints.
    b. She starts crying and shaking.
    c. She asks Jim if he would like to play a game.
    d. She runs away to another room.

14. What are Tom's plans for the future?
    a. He is going back to school to work on his doctorate.
    b. He is planning to move to California to break into the movie business.
    c. He has paid his dues to the Merchant Seaman's Union and plans to leave soon.
    d. He wants to become president of the company where he works, so he works long hours.

15. How does Amanda act towards Jim?
    a. She is rude and sarcastic.
    b. She reverts to her girlish charms and talks incessantly at him.
    c. She ignores Jim and talks at him through Laura.
    d. She is very businesslike and aloof.

16. One of Laura's animals is different from all of the others in the menagerie. It symbolizes that she is different from others, and also has the most delicate character in the family. What animal is it?
    a. It is a swan.
    b. It is a fawn.
    c. It is a butterfly.
    d. It is a unicorn.

17. Jim knows that Laura is very shy and insecure. He tries to make her realize that she is not so different from anyone else. What does he do?
    a. He reads poetry to her.
    b. He takes her out to the fire escape to look at the stars.
    c. He asks her to dance.
    d. He tells her about his own troubled childhood.

The Glass Menagerie Multiple Choice Unit Test 1 Page 4

18. What causes Laura to retreat back into her solitary world.
    a. He tells her he likes her but can't stand Amanda. He says he won't ask her on a date.
    b. Her mother screams at her for kissing Jim.
    c. Jim makes fun of her collection of animals.
    d. Jim confesses that he is to be married to a girl named Betty.

19. Laura sees Jim as a hero with exceptional capabilities. What is Jim actually?
    a. He is an egotistical playboy.
    b. He is a kind, slightly clumsy man who holds an ordinary job.
    c. He is even more heroic and exceptional than she realizes.
    d. He is an unintelligent, rather slovenly bore.

20. Which of these is not a conflict in *The Glass Menagerie*?
    a. illusion versus reality
    b. man versus man
    c. man versus society
    d. man versus nature

The Glass Menagerie Multiple Choice Unit Test 1 Page 5

III. Quotations
   Identify the speaker of the following quotations:

   A=Laura   B=Amanda   C=Tom   D=Jim

1. I haven't enjoyed one bite of this dinner because of your constant directions on how to eat it.

2. I judge you to be an old-fashioned type of girl. Well, I think that's a pretty good type to be.

3. I finally said to him, Tom--good gracious!--why don't you bring this paragon to supper?

4. Yesterday you confiscated my books!

5. I'm all right. I slipped, but I'm all right.

6. My devotion has made me a witch ....

7. You know what I judge to be the trouble with you? Inferiority complex!

8. Only animals have to satisfy instincts! Surely your aims are somewhat higher than theirs!

9. Oh, mother--*you* answer the door!

10. Look at them-- All of those glamorous people--having adventures--hogging it all, gobbling the whole thing up!

11. What are we going to do, what is going to become of us, what is the future?

12. My callers were gentlemen--all!

13. People are not so dreadful when you know them. That's what you have to remember!

14. Man is by instinct a lover, a hunter, a fighter ....

15. Somebody--ought to--*kiss* you, Laura!

16. Things have a way of turning out so badly.

17. Go, then! Go to the moon--you selfish dreamer!

The Glass Menagerie Multiple Choice Unit Test 1 Page 6

III. Composition
    Who is the main character in *The Glass Menagerie*? Defend your choice.

The Glass Menagerie Multiple Choice Unit Test 1 Page 7

IV. Vocabulary

___ 1. Candelabrum   a. Extreme harshness or severity; rigor

___ 2. Archetype   b. Illness usually occurring as a complication of pneumonia

___ 3. Slighted   c. About to happen

___ 4. Matriculating   d. Appeared as one who endures great suffering

___ 5. Intimated   e. Behaving so as to invite or incur

___ 6. Specter   f. One's usual mood; temperament

___ 7. Beleaguered   g. Took

___ 8. Propaganda   h. Chewing

___ 9. Preposterous   i. Made small in size, degree, or amount; lacking

___ 10. Imminent   j. Absurd

___ 11. Pleurosis   k. Hinted; told privately or subtly

___ 12. Rejuvenated   l. A haunting or disturbing image or prospect

___ 13. Disposition   m. A large decorative candlestick with several branches

___ 14. Martyred   n. Support

___ 15. Courting   o. Persuasive material put out by the advocates of a cause

___ 16. Confiscated   p. Made young again

___ 17. Emulate   q. Enrolling

___ 18. Tyranny   r. An original model after which other similar things are patterned; prototype

___ 19. Patronage   s. Harassed by; surrounded by

___ 20. Mastication   t. To try to equal or excel through imitation

MULTIPLE CHOICE UNIT TEST 2 - *The Glass Menagerie*

I. Multiple Choice

1. Laura is the mother of Tom and Amanda. She is worried about her children's future and nags them in an effort to improve their chances for a good position.
    a. True
    b. False

2. Laura wants adventure. She is slightly crippled. She feels like she is nailed up in a coffin.
    a. True
    b. False

3. Tom is shy and frail. Although he is afraid of coping with the outside world, his mother is forcing him to "be a man" and get a job.
    a. True
    b. False

4. Tom explains that there is a specter and a hope hovering over the apartment. What is it?
    a. Laura's father has died and left her a considerable amount of money.
    b. Amanda has decided to let Laura live her own life.
    c. Tom has been offered a better position in another city. They are all going with him.
    d. There are prospects for a gentleman called for Laura.

5. Why doesn't Amanda believe Tom goes to the movies?
    a. She is neurotic and afraid that he secretly has a girlfriend.
    b. She cannot see that it is possible to escape and not come to a bad end.
    c. She has a friend who told her she once saw Tom in a bar when he was supposed to be at the movies.
    d. She thinks it is sinful to waste time, and she doesn't want to believe he is wasting his time and sinning.

6. Who is in the "nailed up coffin" and who found a way out of one?
    a. Tom is in it. His father got out.
    b. Amanda is in it. Laura got out.
    c. Laura is in it. Tom got out.
    d. Laura is in it. Amanda got out.

The Glass Menagerie Multiple Choice Unit Test 2 Page 2

7. Laura cannot deal in any way with the outside world. The thought causes her so much anxiety that she becomes physically sick and weak. How does Williams symbolically show this?
    a. She keeps her glass collection locked up.
    b. She doesn't own a coat, scarf, or gloves since she never goes out.
    c. She leaves the apartment once and slips on the fire escape.
    d. She refuses to use the telephone.

8. Tom and Amanda disagree over what the causes of human action should be. What does Tom think?
    a. Tom thinks that man is the master of his fate.
    b. Tom thinks that man's course in life is predetermined and cannot be controlled or changed.
    c. Tom thinks man should be free to do whatever suits him at a given moment.
    d. Tom thinks man's instinct is that of a hunter, lover and fighter; that these are somehow more purely human drives.

9. What does Amanda think the causes of human actions should be?
    a. Amanda believes basically the same things as Tom. He developed his philosophy from her influences.
    b. Amanda believes people should govern themselves according to principles of the mind and the spirit. She equates passionate feelings with animal filth.
    c. Amanda believes people should act to do anything they can to survive. The end justifies the means.
    d. Amanda is very religious. She believes people should follow the Bible's teachings.

10. What does Amanda ask of Tom?
    a. She wants him to bring a gentleman caller for Laura home from work.
    b. She wants him to start taking her and Laura to church every Sunday.
    c. She wants him to either ask for a raise or get another, better paying job. She wants to move to a larger apartment.
    d. She wants him to find a psychiatrist who can help Laura.

11. What can we gather about Amanda's husband's character? Even though we do not see him in the play, we learn some things about him, things which reflect particularly in Tom and Amanda.
    a. He was kind and sweet and unassuming. He was always trying to please others.
    b. He was sickly and very much an introvert.
    c. He was a hard-driving, career-oriented man who cared little for his family.
    d. He was a good looking charmer who drank a bit too much and followed where his instincts led him.

The Glass Menagerie Multiple Choice Unit Test 2 Page 3

12. Amanda makes both of these statement: "All pretty girls are a trap, a pretty trap, and men expect them to be." "No girl can do worse than put herself at the mercy of a handsome appearance." What do these statements show about her?
    a. She is losing her grip on reality.
    b. She has a double standard.
    c. She has feelings for her children, even though she doesn't express them clearly.
    d. She is a perfectionist.

13. What does Laura do after she opens the door for Tom and Jim.
    a. She runs away to another room.
    b. She starts crying and shaking.
    c. She asks Jim if he would like to play a game.
    d. She faints.

14. What are Tom's plans for the future?
    a. He is going back to school to work on his doctorate.
    b. He has paid his dues to the Merchant Seaman's Union and plans to leave soon.
    c. He is planning to move to California to break into the movie business.
    d. He wants to become president of the company where he works, so he works long hours.

15. How does Amanda act towards Jim?
    a. She reverts to her girlish charms and talks incessantly at him.
    b. She is rude and sarcastic.
    c. She ignores Jim and talks at him through Laura.
    d. She is very businesslike and aloof.

16. One of Laura's animals is different from all of the others in the menagerie. It symbolizes that she is different from others, and also has the most delicate character in the family. What animal is it?
    a. It is a swan.
    b. It is a fawn.
    c. It is a unicorn.
    d. It is a butterfly.

The Glass Menagerie Multiple Choice Unit Test 2 Page 4

17. Jim knows that Laura is very shy and insecure. He tries to make her realize that she is not so different from anyone else. What does he do?
    a. He reads poetry to her.
    b. He takes her out to the fire escape to look at the stars.
    c. He tells her about his own troubled childhood.
    d. He asks her to dance.

18. What causes Laura to retreat back into her solitary world.
    a. He tells her he likes her but can't stand Amanda. He says he won't ask her on a date.
    b. Jim confesses that he is to be married to a girl named Betty.
    c. Jim makes fun of her collection of animals.
    d. Her mother screams at her for kissing Jim.

19. Laura sees Jim as a hero with exceptional capabilities. What is Jim actually?
    a. He is a kind, slightly clumsy man who holds an ordinary job.
    b. He is an egotistical playboy.
    c. He is even more heroic and exceptional than she realizes.
    d. He is an unintelligent, rather slovenly bore.

20. Which of these is not a conflict in *The Glass Menagerie*?
    a. Man versus nature
    b. Man versus man
    c. Man versus society
    d. Illusion versus reality

The Glass Menagerie Multiple Choice Unit Test 2 Page 5

III. Quotations

Identify the speaker of the following quotations:

A=Tom   B=Jim   C=Laura   D=Amanda

1. I haven't enjoyed one bite of this dinner because of your constant directions on how to eat it.

2. I judge you to be an old-fashioned type of girl. Well, I think that's a pretty good type to be.

3. I finally said to him, Tom--good gracious!--why don't you bring this paragon to supper?

4. Yesterday you confiscated my books!

5. I'm all right. I slipped, but I'm all right.

6. My devotion has made me a witch ....

7. You know what I judge to be the trouble with you? Inferiority complex!

8. Only animals have to satisfy instincts! Surely your aims are somewhat higher than theirs!

9. Oh, mother--*you* answer the door!

10. Look at them-- All of those glamorous people--having adventures--hogging it all, gobbling the whole thing up!

11. What are we going to do, what is going to become of us, what is the future?

12. My callers were gentlemen--all!

13. People are not so dreadful when you know them. That's what you have to remember!

14. Man is by instinct a lover, a hunter, a fighter ....

15. Somebody--ought to--*kiss* you, Laura!

16. Things have a way of turning out so badly.

17. Go, then! Go to the moon--you selfish dreamer!

III. Composition

    What is the most important idea presented in *The Glass Menagerie*? Defend your choice.

The Glass Menagerie Multiple Choice Unit Test 2 Page 7

IV. Vocabulary

___ 1. Preposterous   a. One's usual mood; temperament

___ 2. Emissary   b. An agent sent on a mission to represent another

___ 3. Intimated   c. Chewing

___ 4. Candelabrum   d. To try to equal or excel through imitation

___ 5. Confiscated   e. Characterized by persuasive, powerful discourse

___ 6. Menagerie   f. Took

___ 7. Imminent   g. Threatening

___ 8. Matriculating   h. A collection of wild animals on exhibition

___ 9. Negligence   i. Ability; talent

___ 10. Aptitude   j. An original model after which other similar things are patterned; prototype

___ 11. Emulate   k. A visible trace of something that exists no more

___ 12. Archetype   l. About to happen

___ 13. Pleurosis   m. Failure to exercise reasonable care

___ 14. Eloquent   n. Absurd

___ 15. Slighted   o. A haunting or disturbing image or prospect

___ 16. Specter   p. Hinted; told privately or subtly

___ 17. Disposition   q. A large decorative candlestick with several branches

___ 18. Mastication   r. Made small in size, degree, or amount; lacking

___ 19. Ominous   s. Enrolling

___ 20. Vestige   t. Illness usually occurring as a complication of pneumonia

ANSWER SHEET - *The Glass Menagerie*
Multiple Choice Unit Tests

I. Matching	II. Multiple Choice	IV. Vocabulary
1. ___	1. ___	1. ___
2. ___	2. ___	2. ___
3. ___	3. ___	3. ___
4. ___	4. ___	4. ___
5. ___	5. ___	5. ___
6. ___	6. ___	6. ___
7. ___	7. ___	7. ___
8. ___	8. ___	8. ___
9. ___	9. ___	9. ___
10. ___	10. ___	10. ___
11. ___	11. ___	11. ___
12. ___	12. ___	12. ___
13. ___	13. ___	13. ___
14. ___	14. ___	14. ___
15. ___	15. ___	15. ___
16. ___	16. ___	16. ___
17. ___	17. ___	17. ___
18. ___		18. ___
19. ___		19. ___
20. ___		20. ___

ANSWER KEY - *The Glass Menagerie*
Multiple Choice Unit Tests

Answers to Unit Test 1 are in the left column. Answers to Unit Test 2 are in the right column.

I. Matching	II. Multiple Choice	IV. Vocabulary
1. A B	1. C A	1. M B
2. B B	2. D B	2. R N
3. B B	3. B D	3. I P
4. B D	4. C A	4. Q Q
5. C B	5. A C	5. K F
6. C A	6. B D	6. L H
7. D C	7. D B	7. S L
8. C D	8. B D	8. O S
9. A B	9. A C	9. J M
10. C A	10. C A	10. C I
11. B D	11. B D	11. B D
12. D B	12. B D	12. P J
13. D A	13. D B	13. F T
14. C B	14. C A	14. D E
15. B A	15. D B	15. E R
16. D C	16. B D	16. G O
17. C D	17. B D	17. T A
18. D B		18. A C
19. B A		19. N G
20. D A		20. H K

UNIT RESOURCE MATERIALS

BULLETIN BOARD IDEAS - *The Glass Menagerie*

1. Save one corner of the board for the best of students' *The Glass Menagerie* writing assignments.

2. Take one of the word search puzzles from the extra activities section and with a marker copy it over in a large size on the bulletin board. Write the clue words to find to one side. Invite students prior to and after class to find the words and circle them on the bulletin board.

3. Write several of the most significant quotations from the book onto the board on brightly colored paper.

4. Make a bulletin board listing the vocabulary words for this unit. As you complete sections of the novel and discuss the vocabulary for each section, write the definitions on the bulletin board. (If your board is one students face frequently, it will help them learn the words.)

5. Title the board: THE GLASS MENAGERIE: POSITIVE WAYS TO ESCAPE. On the bulletin board place pictures of ways people find to escape the pressures of daily life without resorting to drugs and alcohol.

6. Title the board THE GLASS MENAGERIE: LIVING WITH A HANDICAP. Find pictures of people with all kinds of handicaps. The pictures should show the people finding a way to make the best of their situations. Do everything from people who have to wear eye glasses or hearing aids to those who have more severe physical handicaps.

7. Title the board SELF-CONFIDENCE: CREATE A POSITIVE FUTURE FOR YOURSELF. Post encouraging slogans--like the ones you find in *Reader's Digest* or on calendars--little tips and guides to help people be better, more confident people.

8. Title the board THE GLASS MENAGERIE: THINGS MOMS SAY AND DO. As an introductory activity to the unit, have students take colored markers and write up things their mothers say and do that are typical "mom" kinds of things.

EXTRA ACTIVITIES - *The Glass Menagerie*

One of the difficulties in teaching a novel is that all students don't read at the same speed. One student who likes to read may take the book home and finish it in a day or two. Sometimes a few students finish the in-class assignments early. The problem, then, is finding suitable extra activities for students.

One thing you can do is to keep a little library in the classroom. For this unit on *The Glass Menagerie*, you might check out from the school library other related books and articles about psychology, diseases that cause handicaps, current issues facing handicapped people, career opportunities of all kinds, information about different kinds of hobbies, and positive ways to escape the daily pressures of life without using drugs or alcohol.

Other things you may keep on hand are puzzles. We have made some relating directly to *The Glass Menagerie* for you. Feel free to duplicate them.

Some students may like to draw. You might devise a contest or allow some extra-credit grade for students who draw characters or scenes from The Glass Menagerie. Note, too, that if the students do not want to keep their drawings you may pick up some extra bulletin board materials this way. If you have a contest and you supply the prize (a CD or something like that perhaps), you could, possibly, make the drawing itself a non-refundable entry fee.

The pages which follow contain games, puzzles and worksheets. The keys, when appropriate, immediately follow the puzzle or worksheet. There are two main groups of activities: one group for the unit; that is, generally relating to the *Glass Menagerie* text, and another group of activities related strictly to the *Glass Menagerie* vocabulary.

Directions for these games, puzzles and worksheets are self-explanatory. The object here is to provide you with extra materials you may use in any way you choose.

MORE ACTIVITIES - *The Glass Menagerie*

1. Have your students act out the play in front of a couple of other classes of students. Be sure to invite your yearbook and newspaper photographers. You can get additional bulletin board materials for future use, and your students can get recognition for their work.

2. Use some of the related topics noted earlier for an in-class library as topics for research papers or guest speakers.

3. Have students develop their own plans for the future, as Amanda tried to get Laura to do, and as Tom eventually did for himself.

4. Have students design a playbill or book cover for *The Glass Menagerie*.

5. Have students design a bulletin board (ready to be put up; not just sketched) for *The Glass Menagerie*.

6. Do a mini unit about careers. Have your guidance office supply you with materials, and show students what careers are available after they graduate.

7. Use costumes and props when you do your oral readings to make it more like a real production.

WORD SEARCH - *The Glass Menagerie*

All words in this list are associated with *The Glass Menagerie*. The words are placed backwards, forward, diagonally, up and down. The included words are listed below the word searches.

```
Y C Y P S F V A Y H S L B A D C G Z Z J K K R B
R H G M A Z S T P E D E A J M A V Q S M I M E N
T H I M E L O H S A N L Y U N A U O A S I T L S
U N I C O R N O V E R B E A R I N G S J T O M N
D L N B O N R W C E T T M I N A A D H Y R A M G
Y A M D A F Z S N P C E M S F Z J B A T I D G P
D Y N M F B F N M Q L N T E I G T B N L E D H E
S F A A C T I I V T M I E N N E N O L G K R R D
J E I S K D T K N X N I E R G T C I R B L E P N
S R H R B V C E X C R S Z E W J W Q W Q H A M C
T T M Y E G G L T E R F L X Y A L X K T S T S Q
Y L Y B S B V H G K W L K D R L L X O R V N X S
W R Y K D Z D A N R O X S N M H S M G D P C T W
Z L R Z Q Y N Z M C G L H F L Z M G Q N W R M V
T G L B J E T M S Q Y B J G P D Z X C W K K D D
C C T H M B N W W K J X P X M Q B S P H R K P X
J T Q V G L G K V S Y S R J N F M R G Y Y X P Z
```

ACT	FAMILY	MENAGERIE	TEST
AMANDA	FIRE	MIND	TOM
APARTMENT	GENTLEMAN	MOTHER	TRAP
BETTY	GLASS	OVERBEARING	UNICORN
COFFIN	INSTINCT	ROSES	WILLIAMS
COLLEGE	JIM	SCENE	WINGFIELD
CONTROL	KISS	SEAMAN	ZOO
DANCE	LAURA	SON	DAUGHTER
LAWRENCE	STAGE	DINNER	MAGAZINES
SYMBOLS			

KEY: WORD SEARCH - *The Glass Menagerie*

All words in this list are associated with *The Glass Menagerie*. The words are placed backwards, forward, diagonally, up and down. The included words are listed below the word searches.

```
              F   A     S   L   A D               K   B
          M A Z S T P E D E A   M A       S M I M E
          I M E L O   S A N L   U N A U O A S I T L S
U N I C O R N O V E R B E A R I N G S J T O M
D L N B O N R   C E T T M I N A A D H Y R A
Y A M   A F   S N   C E M S F Z     A T I   G
D Y   M     F N     L N T E I G     N L E       E
S F A A C T I I   T   I E N N E N O L G   R R
    E I     D     N   N I E R G T C I     L E
S     R       E   C R S   E W   W   W   H A
        E   G   T E     L     A       T       S
              G     L           L   O             S
            A     O               M
          N     C
        E
      M
```

ACT	FAMILY	MENAGERIE	TEST
AMANDA	FIRE	MIND	TOM
APARTMENT	GENTLEMAN	MOTHER	TRAP
BETTY	GLASS	OVERBEARING	UNICORN
COFFIN	INSTINCT	ROSES	WILLIAMS
COLLEGE	JIM	SCENE	WINGFIELD
CONTROL	KISS	SEAMAN	ZOO
DANCE	LAURA	SON	DAUGHTER
LAWRENCE	STAGE	DINNER	MAGAZINES
SYMBOLS			

CROSSWORD - *The Glass Menagerie*

CROSSWORD CLUES - *The Glass Menagerie*

ACROSS
1. Amanda hopes for ---- callers for Laura
5. Jim asks Laura to do this
8. Tom has paid his dues to the Merchant ---'s Union
10. Amanda, Tom and Laura together
12. Tom to Amanda
14. He hates his job and wants adventure
16. Amanda thinks causes of human action come from this
18. Play division
19. Jim's fiancee`
20. Breakfast food
23. Tom feels as if he is in a nailed up one
25. Jim was a --- of the Wingfields
26. Place Laura liked to go instead of school
27. Act division
28. Leased
30. Jim called Laura Blue --- by mistake
31. Not ever
35. Amanda wants to ---- Tom
38. Glass ----
40. Laura to Amanda
41. Aid
42. Author of Tom's novel Amanda returned to the library

DOWN
1. ---- Menagerie
2. Laura became physically ill during her first speed ----
3. Make able to
4. Setting of the play
6. Mother of Tom and Laura
7. Things that represent other things or have double meanings
9. The gentleman caller
11. Tom thinks causes of human action come from this
13. Adjective to describe Amanda
15. Amanda sold these to make extra money
17. Place where plays are performed
21. Jim gives Laura one to make her realize she is pretty and appealing
22. Boyfriends
23. Laura quit business ----
24. Laura slipped on the ---- escape
29. Laura was too sick to eat it
32. Amanda to Laura and Tom
33. Amanda and Tom never --- about anything; concur
34. 'All pretty girls are a ---, a pretty
36. Impolite
37. She can't deal with the outside world
39. Past participle of 'to see'

CROSSWORD ANSWER KEY - *The Glass Menagerie*

MATCHING QUIZ/WORKSHEET 1 - *The Glass Menagerie*

___ 1. FAMILY   A. Adjective to describe Amanda

___ 2. ACT   B. *Glass* ----

___ 3. LAWRENCE   C. Author of *The Glass Menagerie*

___ 4. GENTLEMAN   D. Jim's fiancee`

___ 5. OVERBEARING   E. Play division

___ 6. DAUGHTER   F. Laura's last name

___ 7. ZOO   G. Laura quit business ----

___ 8. TRAP   H. She can't deal with the outside world

___ 9. DINNER   I. Amanda hopes for ---- callers for Laura

___ 10. COLLEGE   J. 'All pretty girls are a ---, a pretty ----'

___ 11. TOM   K. Place Laura liked to go instead of school

___ 12. LAURA   L. Author of Tom's novel Amanda returned to the library

___ 13. JIM   M. Laura was too sick to eat it

___ 14. BETTY   N. Tom to Amanda

___ 15. MAGAZINES   O. Amanda sold these to make extra money

___ 16. SON   P. Laura slipped on the ---- escape

___ 17. WINGFIELD   Q. He hates his job and wants adventure

___ 18. FIRE   R. The gentleman caller

___ 19. WILLIAMS   S. Laura to Amanda

___ 20. MENAGERIE   T. Amanda, Tom and Laura together

KEY: MATCHING QUIZ/WORKSHEET 1 - *The Glass Menagerie*

_T_	1. FAMILY	A. Adjective to describe Amanda
_E_	2. ACT	B. *Glass* ----
_L_	3. LAWRENCE	C. Author of *The Glass Menagerie*
_I_	4. GENTLEMAN	D. Jim's fiancee`
_A_	5. OVERBEARING	E. Play division
_S_	6. DAUGHTER	F. Laura's last name
_K_	7. ZOO	G. Laura quit business ----
_J_	8. TRAP	H. She can't deal with the outside world
_M_	9. DINNER	I. Amanda hopes for ---- callers for Laura
_G_	10. COLLEGE	J. 'All pretty girls are a ---, a pretty ----'
_Q_	11. TOM	K. Place Laura liked to go instead of school
_H_	12. LAURA	L. Author of Tom's novel Amanda returned to the library
_R_	13. JIM	M. Laura was too sick to eat it
_D_	14. BETTY	N. Tom to Amanda
_O_	15. MAGAZINES	O. Amanda sold these to make extra money
_N_	16. SON	P. Laura slipped on the ---- escape
_F_	17. WINGFIELD	Q. He hates his job and wants adventure
_P_	18. FIRE	R. The gentleman caller
_C_	19. WILLIAMS	S. Laura to Amanda
_B_	20. MENAGERIE	T. Amanda, Tom and Laura together

MATCHING QUIZ/WORKSHEET 2 - *The Glass Menagerie*

___ 1. STAGE   A. Place where plays are performed

___ 2. MOTHER   B. Amanda wants to ---- Tom

___ 3. MIND   C. Amanda sold these to make extra money

___ 4. MENAGERIE   D. Things that represent other things or have double meanings

___ 5. SON   E. 'All pretty girls are a ---, a pretty ----'

___ 6. SCENE   F. Laura to Amanda

___ 7. GLASS   G. Setting of the play

___ 8. DAUGHTER   H. Act division

___ 9. DANCE   I. Amanda thinks causes of human action come from this

___ 10. CONTROL   J. Tom has paid his dues to the Merchant ---'s Union

___ 11. SYMBOLS   K. Amanda hopes for ---- callers for Laura

___ 12. DINNER   L. Jim asks Laura to do this

___ 13. SEAMAN   M. The gentleman caller

___ 14. TRAP   N. Symbol for Laura

___ 15. FAMILY   O. Tom to Amanda

___ 16. MAGAZINES   P. Amanda to Laura and Tom

___ 17. UNICORN   Q. *Glass* ----

___ 18. APARTMENT   R. ---- *Menagerie*

___ 19. JIM   S. Amanda, Tom and Laura together

___ 20. GENTLEMAN   T. Laura was too sick to eat it

KEY: MATCHING QUIZ/WORKSHEET 2 - *The Glass Menagerie*

_A_	1. STAGE	A. Place where plays are performed
_P_	2. MOTHER	B. Amanda wants to ---- Tom
_I_	3. MIND	C. Amanda sold these to make extra money
_Q_	4. MENAGERIE	D. Things that represent other things or have double meanings
_O_	5. SON	E. 'All pretty girls are a ---, a pretty ----'
_H_	6. SCENE	F. Laura to Amanda
_R_	7. GLASS	G. Setting of the play
_F_	8. DAUGHTER	H. Act division
_L_	9. DANCE	I. Amanda thinks causes of human action come from this
_B_	10. CONTROL	J. Tom has paid his dues to the Merchant ---'s Union
_D_	11. SYMBOLS	K. Amanda hopes for ---- callers for Laura
_T_	12. DINNER	L. Jim asks Laura to do this
_J_	13. SEAMAN	M. The gentleman caller
_E_	14. TRAP	N. Symbol for Laura
_S_	15. FAMILY	O. Tom to Amanda
_C_	16. MAGAZINES	P. Amanda to Laura and Tom
_N_	17. UNICORN	Q. *Glass* ----
_G_	18. APARTMENT	R. ---- *Menagerie*
_M_	19. JIM	S. Amanda, Tom and Laura together
_K_	20. GENTLEMAN	T. Laura was too sick to eat it

JUGGLE LETTER REVIEW GAME CLUE SHEET - *The Glass Menagerie*

SCRAMBLED	WORD	CLUE
EIREEMAGN	MENAGERIE	*Glass* _____
MJI	JIM	The Gentleman caller
ORSSE	ROSES	Jim called Laura Blue _____ by mistake
EDCAN	DANCE	Jim asks Laura to do this
DNEIILGWF	WINGFIELD	Laura's last name
NSO	SON	Tom to Amanda
MNASAE	SEAMAN	Tom has paid his dues to the Merchant _____'s Union
SKSI	KISS	Jim gives Laura one to make her realize she is pretty and appealing
RLCOTON	CONTROL	Amanda wants to _____ Tom
NITTCNSI	INSTINCT	Tom thinks causes of human action come from this
AANDAM	AMANDA	Mother of Tom and Laura
ISIAMLWL	WILLIAMS	Author of The Glass Menagerie
ARAUL	LAURA	She can't deal with the outside world
TAC	ACT	Play division
OHMRTE	MOTHER	Amanda to Laura and Tom
ELNEAMTGN	GENTLEMAN	Amanda hopes for _____ callers for Laura
OMT	TOM	He hates his job and wants adventure
ZMAEGSINA	MAGAZINES	Amanda sold these to make extra money
EESCN	SCENE	Act division
TTEYB	BETTY	Jim's fiancee`
PART	TRAP	'All pretty girls are a _____, a pretty _____'
NUCORNI	UNICORN	Symbol for Laura
ASSLG	GLASS	_____ Menagerie
ETTS	TEST	Laura became physically ill during her first speed _____
OOZ	ZOO	Place Laura liked to go instead of school
AENEIBVRORGR	OVERBEARING	Adjective to describe Amanda
BOLMSYS	SYMBOLS	Things that represent other things or have double meanings
MTTAPNREA	APARTMENT	Setting of the play
DNIM	MIND	Amanda thinks causes of human action come from this
MLYFIA	FAMILY	Amanda, Tom and Laura together
NIOFFC	COFFIN	Tom feels as if he is in a nailed up one
ERIF	FIRE	Amanda slipped on the _____ escape
GLECLEO	COLLEGE	Laura quit business _____

VOCABULARY RESOURCE MATERIALS

VOCABULARY WORD SEARCH - *The Glass Menagerie*

All words in this list are associated with *The Glass Menagerie* with an emphasis on the vocabulary words chosen for study in the text. The words are placed backwards, forward, diagonally, up and down. The included words are listed below.

```
L M R T N S S H J J Q X L B N D Q X T B E Z P V
F Y A S N X R A K C D T I C G O Z D L D T L P N
T F Y S M E E X T J T N V E W W I F U H P E S B
C O U R T I N G N I T A L U C I R T A M I P L P
K J M C A I H I I R Y G P C N I D P R R R Z Y
R Y E I C S C V M T N I R K E T E X E E K G K F
R P N B N V S A M M S W C A P G F G P Q C P J Z
S E J O B O T I T A I E P A N J A O I E X E R B
A R J S I E U D M I R R V L L N S N L L Y Z D Z
K R V U D T E S C E O T M L E T Y O O R G F F F
X V C H V T I F L P V N Y M E U Q R N R E E J B
B G L H H E V S A M V D L R X U R G S T T D N V
C F B G E P N G O D D J O H E Z W O A W M A B V
Y N I P K T A A C P N U J N V D G L S Z G G P Q
B L W Q M N Y M T S S N T K Q S U L W I T K B P
S G P Z D B L P K E S I K S L M F F Q L S C S M
H K L A W R M G E P D C D B E L E A G U E R E D
```

APTITUDE	EMISSARY	MENAGERIE	REJUVENATED
ARCHETYPE	EMULATE	NEGLIGENCE	SATIRICAL
BELEAGUERED	IMMINENT	OMINOUS	SLIGHTED
COURTING	INTIMATED	PATRONAGE	SPECTER
DECEPTION	MARTYRED	PLEUROSIS	TYRANNY
DISPOSITION	MASTICATION	PREPOSTEROUS	VESTIGE
ELOQUENT	MATRICULATING	PROPAGANDA	

KEY: VOCABULARY WORD SEARCH - *The Glass Menagerie*

All words in this list are associated with *The Glass Menagerie* with an emphasis on the vocabulary words chosen for study in the text. The words are placed backwards, forward, diagonally, up and down. The included words are listed below.

```
        M     T     S                    N              E
        A  N  R  A        I     O        D
        Y S  E  E  T     N  E.  I  U        E
   C O U R T  I  N  G  N I T A L U C I R T A M I P
        M C  A  I     I I R Y     N I     P R R
        E I  S  C     M T   I R   E T E     E E
   R P  N    N  S  A  M M S   C A P G   G P   C
   S E  O    O  T  I  T A I E P A N   A O I E   E
   A    J    I  E  U  D M I R R V L L N S N L L     D
        R    U  D  T  E S   E O T   E T Y O O   G
        C    V  T  I     P   N Y M E U Q   R E E
             H  H  E  S  A        R   U R   T T   N
             G  E     N  G O        O   E     O A     A
             I        T  A A   P   U   N   D   L S       P
        L             N  Y T     S   T         U     I
   S             D    P     E    I         M       S
             A              E    D    D B E L E A G U E R E D
```

APTITUDE	EMISSARY	MENAGERIE	REJUVENATED
ARCHETYPE	EMULATE	NEGLIGENCE	SATIRICAL
BELEAGUERED	IMMINENT	OMINOUS	SLIGHTED
COURTING	INTIMATED	PATRONAGE	SPECTER
DECEPTION	MARTYRED	PLEUROSIS	TYRANNY
DISPOSITION	MASTICATION	PREPOSTEROUS	VESTIGE
ELOQUENT	MATRICULATING	PROPAGANDA	

VOCABULARY CROSSWORD - *The Glass Menagerie*

VOCABULARY CROSSWORD CLUES - *The Glass Menagerie*

ACROSS
2. Chewing
6. Amanda thinks causes of human action come from this
7. Laura was a bit ---; unusual; different
9. She can't deal with the outside world
11. Extreme harshness or severity; rigor
12. A haunting or disturbing image or prospect
14. Failure to exercise reasonable care
16. Look with eyes
17. 'All pretty girls are a ---, a pretty ----'
19. Laura slipped on the ---- escape
20. Jim --- on the floor
21. One who tells an untruth
22. Act division
23. To try to equal or excel through imitation
29. Enrolling
31. Coordinating conjunction
32. Fuel for cars
33. Given to complaining; peevish
35. Laura became physically ill during her first speed ----
37. A visible trace of something that exists no more
38. Tom to Amanda
40. Place where plays are performed
42. Support
44. Took
45. The gentleman caller
46. Begin

DOWN
1. To dwell on; nag; ---- on
2. Appeared as one who endures great suffering
3. About to happen
4. An original model after which other similar things are patterned; prototype
5. Hinted; told privately or subtly
6. A collection of wild animals on exhibition
8. Jim asks Laura to do this
10. A ruse; a trick
12. Made small in size, degree, or amount; lacking
13. Jim called Laura Blue --- by mistake
15. Behaving so as to invite or incur
18. Illness usually occurring as a complication of pneumonia
24. Ability; talent
25. An agent sent on a mission to represent another
26. Persuasive material put out by the advocates of a cause
27. Play division
28. Characterized by persuasive, powerful discourse
30. Definite article
32. ---- Menagerie
34. Threatening
36. Jim gives Laura one to make her realize she is pretty and appealing
39. Jim's fiancee`
41. Amanda was a --- mother; she just nagged too much. Opposite of bad
43. He hates his job and wants adventure

VOCABULARY CROSSWORD ANSWER KEY - *The Glass Menagerie*

VOCABULARY WORKSHEET 1 - *The Glass Menagerie*

___ 1. CANDELABRUM   A. Extreme harshness or severity; rigor

___ 2. ARCHETYPE   B. Illness usually occurring as a complication of pneumonia

___ 3. SLIGHTED   C. About to happen

___ 4. MATRICULATING   D. Appeared as one who endures great suffering

___ 5. INTIMATED   E. Behaving so as to invite or incur

___ 6. SPECTER   F. One's usual mood; temperament

___ 7. BELEAGUERED   G. Took

___ 8. PROPAGANDA   H. Chewing

___ 9. PREPOSTEROUS   I. Made small in size, degree, or amount; lacking

___ 10. IMMINENT   J. Absurd

___ 11. PLEUROSIS   K. Hinted; told privately or subtly

___ 12. REJUVENATED   L. A haunting or disturbing image or prospect

___ 13. DISPOSITION   M. A large decorative candlestick with several branches

___ 14. MARTYRED   N. Support

___ 15. COURTING   O. Persuasive material put out by the advocates of a cause

___ 16. CONFISCATED   P. Made young again

___ 17. EMULATE   Q. Enrolling

___ 18. TYRANNY   R. An original model after which other similar things are patterned; prototype

___ 19. PATRONAGE   S. Harassed by; surrounded by

___ 20. MASTICATION   T. To try to equal or excel through imitation

KEY: VOCABULARY WORKSHEET 1 - *The Glass Menagerie*

M   1. CANDELABRUM   A. Extreme harshness or severity; rigor

R   2. ARCHETYPE   B. Illness usually occurring as a complication of pneumonia

I   3. SLIGHTED   C. About to happen

Q   4. MATRICULATING   D. Appeared as one who endures great suffering

K   5. INTIMATED   E. Behaving so as to invite or incur

L   6. SPECTER   F. One's usual mood; temperament

S   7. BELEAGUERED   G. Took

O   8. PROPAGANDA   H. Chewing

J   9. PREPOSTEROUS   I. Made small in size, degree, or amount; lacking

C   10. IMMINENT   J. Absurd

B   11. PLEUROSIS   K. Hinted; told privately or subtly

P   12. REJUVENATED   L. A haunting or disturbing image or prospect

F   13. DISPOSITION   M. A large decorative candlestick with several branches

D   14. MARTYRED   N. Support

E   15. COURTING   O. Persuasive material put out by the advocates of a cause

G   16. CONFISCATED   P. Made young again

T   17. EMULATE   Q. Enrolling

A   18. TYRANNY   R. An original model after which other similar things are patterned; prototype

N   19. PATRONAGE   S. Harassed by; surrounded by

H   20. MASTICATION   T. To try to equal or excel through imitation

VOCABULARY WORKSHEET 2 - *The Glass Menagerie*

___ 1. Given to complaining; peevish
    a. Menagerie   b. Archetype   c. Negligence   d. Querulous

___ 2. Enrolling
    a. Preposterous   b. Matriculating   c. Archetype   d. Menagerie

___ 3. Ability; talent
    a. Disposition   b. Aptitude   c. Ominous   d. Satirical

___ 4. Using irony, sarcasm, or caustic wit to attack or expose folly, vice or stupidity
    a. Slighted   b. Archetype   c. Menagerie   d. Satirical

___ 5. Took
    a. Confiscated   b. Intimated   c. Imminent   d. Rejuvenated

___ 6. Absurd
    a. Preposterous   b. Mastication   c. Matriculating   d. Rejuvenated

___ 7. Chewing
    a. Tyranny   b. Patronage   c. Preposterous   d. Mastication

___ 8. About to happen
    a. Aptitude   b. Imminent   c. Confiscated   d. Disposition

___ 9. Persuasive material put out by the advocates of a cause
    a. Candelabrum   b. Slighted   c. Propaganda   d. Matriculating

___ 10. Support
    a. Mastication   b. Patronage   c. Tyranny   d. Beleaguered

___ 11. To try to equal or excel through imitation
    a. Matriculating   b. Slighted   c. Specter   d. Emulate

___ 12. A visible trace of something that exists no more
    a. Imminent   b. Specter   c. Satirical   d. Vestige

___ 13. A haunting or disturbing image or prospect
    a. Matriculating   b. Patronage   c. Specter   d. Aptitude

___ 14. Threatening
    a. Ominous   b. Confiscated   c. Aptitude   d. Disposition

___ 15. One's usual mood; temperament
    a. Aptitude   b. Deception   c. Disposition   d. Vestige

___ 16. Appeared as one who endures great suffering
    a. Martyred   b. Tyranny   c. Emulate   d. Specter

___ 17. Made young again
    a. Pleurosis   b. Rejuvenated   c. Tyranny   d. Mastication

___ 18. Hinted; told privately or subtly
    a. Intimated   b. Specter   c. Vestige   d. Imminent

___ 19. An original model after which other similar things are patterned; prototype
    a. Archetype   b. Martyred   c. Intimated   d. Emulate

___ 20. Behaving so as to invite or incur
    a. Vestige   b. Aptitude   c. Eloquent   d. Courting

KEY: VOCABULARY WORKSHEET 2 - *The Glass Menagerie*

__D__ 1. Given to complaining; peevish
    a. Menagerie   b. Archetype   c. Negligence   d. Querulous

__B__ 2. Enrolling
    a. Preposterous   b. Matriculating   c. Archetype   d. Menagerie

__B__ 3. Ability; talent
    a. Disposition   b. Aptitude   c. Ominous   d. Satirical

__D__ 4. Using irony, sarcasm, or caustic wit to attack or expose folly, vice or stupidity
    a. Slighted   b. Archetype   c. Menagerie   d. Satirical

__A__ 5. Took
    a. Confiscated   b. Intimated   c. Imminent   d. Rejuvenated

__A__ 6. Absurd
    a. Preposterous   b. Mastication   c. Matriculating   d. Rejuvenated

__D__ 7. Chewing
    a. Tyranny   b. Patronage   c. Preposterous   d. Mastication

__B__ 8. About to happen
    a. Aptitude   b. Imminent   c. Confiscated   d. Disposition

__C__ 9. Persuasive material put out by the advocates of a cause
    a. Candelabrum   b. Slighted   c. Propaganda   d. Matriculating

__B__ 10. Support
    a. Mastication   b. Patronage   c. Tyranny   d. Beleaguered

__D__ 11. To try to equal or excel through imitation
    a. Matriculating   b. Slighted   c. Specter   d. Emulate

__D__ 12. A visible trace of something that exists no more
    a. Imminent   b. Specter   c. Satirical   d. Vestige

__C__ 13. A haunting or disturbing image or prospect
    a. Matriculating   b. Patronage   c. Specter   d. Aptitude

__A__ 14. Threatening
    a. Ominous   b. Confiscated   c. Aptitude   d. Disposition

__C__ 15. One's usual mood; temperament
    a. Aptitude   b. Deception   c. Disposition   d. Vestige

__A__ 16. Appeared as one who endures great suffering
    a. Martyred   b. Tyranny   c. Emulate   d. Specter

__B__ 17. Made young again
    a. Pleurosis   b. Rejuvenated   c. Tyranny   d. Mastication

__A__ 18. Hinted; told privately or subtly
    a. Intimated   b. Specter   c. Vestige   d. Imminent

__A__ 19. An original model after which other similar things are patterned; prototype
    a. Archetype   b. Martyred   c. Intimated   d. Emulate

__D__ 20. Behaving so as to invite or incur
    a. Vestige   b. Aptitude   c. Eloquent   d. Courting

VOCABULARY JUGGLE LETTER REVIEW GAME CLUES - *The Glass Menagerie*

SCRAMBLED	WORD	CLUE
AECNMURLADB	CANDELABRUM	A large decorative candlestick with several branches
UGRBEALDEEE	BELEAGUERED	Harassed by; surrounded by
YEECHARTP	ARCHETYPE	An original model after which other similar things are patterned; prototype
OCNUGTRI	COURTING	Behaving so as to invite or incur
HGESTDLI	SLIGHTED	Made small in size, degree, or amount; lacking
EOUEOTSPPSRR	PREPOSTEROUS	Absurd
USSREILOP	PLEUROSIS	Illness usually occurring as a complication of pneumonia
ADNAGPRAOP	PROPAGANDA	Persuasive material put out by the advocates of a cause
CIEPNOETD	DECEPTION	A ruse; a trick
ETINMMIN	IMMINENT	About to happen
RQSUEOLUU	QUERULOUS	Given to complaining; peevish
DTAETIPU	APTITUDE	Ability; talent
GMENERIEA	MENAGERIE	A collection of wild animals on exhibition
RTPSECE	SPECTER	A haunting or disturbing image or prospect
ERENDTAUVEJ	REJUVENATED	Made young again
TNMAAOIICST	MASTICATION	Chewing
SDTNOCACEFI	CONFISCATED	Took
NNYTAYR	TYRANNY	Extreme harshness or severity; rigor
YRSSEMIA	EMISSARY	An agent sent on a mission to represent another
MAETNIDTI	INTIMATED	Hinted; told privately or subtly
UEETLMA	EMULATE	To try to equal or excel through imitation
IOMUOSN	OMINOUS	Threatening
EGECNNELGI	NEGLIGENCE	Failure to exercise reasonable care
EOLNQETU	ELOQUENT	Characterized by persuasive, powerful discourse
TAAPREGON	PATRONAGE	Support
GVTESEI	VESTIGE	A visible trace of something that exists no more
OPOIDISNTIS	DISPOSITION	One's usual mood; temperament
TCLRASAII	SATIRICAL	Using irony, sarcasm, or caustic wit to attack or expose folly, vice or stupidity

www.ingramcontent.com/pod-product-compliance
Lightning Source LLC
Chambersburg PA
CBHW051417070526
44584CB00023B/3463